"Using accessible analogies and clear steps, John Barcanic leads you to a deeper understanding of the long-game of truly trusting God. His four main questions are a brilliant reduction, down to its essence, of life questions that plague the human race. This book will speak to new Christians and those who have been on a lifelong journey with Christ."
—Rachel K Shannon, PhD, Licensed Marriage and Family Therapist

"Our world can be a scary, challenging, even chaotic place. How can we rightly navigate our world so that fear does not consume us? John Barcanic draws upon his deep knowledge of the Scriptures and his personal experiences to show us that the only way we can overcome fear is through cultivating "God-confidence. God-confidence takes seriously the challenges of our personal lives and world but shows us how to trust in the greater goodness of God. Eminently practical, biblically faithful, and filled with enjoyable and often humorous stories – this book provides its readers with the resources needed to live a life of faith and flourishing."
—Joshua Jipp, PhD, Associate Professor of New Testament, Trinity Evangelical Divinity School

"In our selfie driven society, "God-Confidence" shares the secret of exchanging our self-confidence for God-confidence. This book will challenge you and give you practical tools to walk in confidence! Through his personal experience, engaging analogies, and Scriptural insights, John Barcanic invites you into a journey of transformation."
—Tre Moore, National Director, India Rural Evangelical Fellowship-USA

"John Barcanic lives what he teaches. He's a tremendous communicator with a lot to say about walking confidently ... in God. Read this book. You'll be glad you did. I know. I was."
—Tom Kraeuter, Author, Bible Teacher

**ALSO AVAILABLE**

*Meaning: Cultivate a Life of Joy, Purpose, and Impact*
*Uncertain Seas: Thrive in the Midst of the Unknown*
*The God-confidence Playbook*

# GOD CONFIDENCE

Cultivating Courageous Faith in Jesus Christ

John Barcanic

A Division of Innovative Ministries International

© 2020 by John Barcanic. All rights reserved.

This publication or any portion thereof may not be reproduced or used in any manner whatsoever without the express written permission of the publisher.

**Intersekt**
A division of Innovative Ministries International
224.858.8843
info@intersekt.org
www.intersekt.org

ISBN E-book edition: 978-0-578-76478-8
ISBN Print book edition: 978-0-578-76477-1

Cover photo by Adele Payman on Unsplash
Cover design supervision by Lyn Barcanic

Limit of Liability/Disclaimer of Warranty:
While the publisher and author have used their best efforts in preparing this book, they make no representations or warranties with respect to the accuracy or completenes of the contents of this book and specifically disclaim any implied warranties of merchantability or fitness for a particular purpose. no warranty may be created or extended by sales representatives or written sales materials. The advice and strategies contained herein may not be suitable for your situation. You should consult with a professional where appropriate. Neither the publisher nor author shall be liable for any loss of profit or any other commercial damages, including but not limited to special, incidental, consequential, or other damages.

Unless otherwise indicated, all scripture quotations are from The ESV® Bible (The Holy Bible, English Standard Version®), copyright © 2001 by Crossway, a publishing ministry of Good News Publishers. Used by permission. All rights reserved.

Scripture quotations marked (NIV) are taken from the Holy Bible, New International Version®, NIV®. Copyright © 1973, 1978, 1984, 2011 by Biblica, Inc.™ Used by permission of Zondervan. All rights reserved worldwide. www.zondervan.com The "NIV" and "New International Version" are trademarks registered in the United States Patent and Trademark Office by Biblica, Inc.™

Printed in the United States of America

I gratefully dedicate this book to Laura Kelly, who was the first to say, "I'd read a book like that. I think a lot of people could be helped by that kind of book."

# CONTENTS

Introduction ... 1

## SECTION 1: THE FOUR REQUIREMENTS OF GOD-CONFIDENCE

1. Confidence Requires Perfection ... 9
2. Confidence Requires Discernment ... 19
3. Confidence Requires Fear ... 37
4. Confidence Requires Stress ... 49

## SECTION 2: GOD'S GOODNESS

5. God Sacrificed for Us ... 61
6. God GRACED Us ... 77
7. God Provides for Us ... 87
8. God Rewards Us ... 99

## SECTION 3: GOD'S GREATNESS

9. Creation ... 111
10. Salvation ... 119
11. Declaration ... 131

## CONTENTS

### SECTION 4: PUTTING IT ALL TOGETHER

| | | |
|---|---|---|
| 12 | The Estate | 151 |
| 13 | Ensure You Understand the Game | 155 |
| 14 | Watch Game Tape | 159 |
| 15 | Drill the Fundamentals | 167 |
| 16 | Practice Specific Plays | 175 |
| 17 | Make In-Game Adjustments | 183 |
| 18 | Build On What Works | 191 |
| 19 | Share Your Love for Winning | 197 |
| 20 | The 10-Step Gameplan | 201 |

| | |
|---|---|
| *Appendix: Additional Resources* | 207 |
| *Acknowledgments* | 209 |
| *About John Barcanic* | 210 |
| *About Intersekt* | 211 |
| *End Notes* | 213 |

# INTRODUCTION

My face flushed with the heat of shame as I stood in the middle of my 16th floor hotel room in downtown Baltimore. The view over the city that evening was beautiful, but I hardly noticed the twinkling lights, the tall buildings, and the little piece of the Inner Harbor I earlier imagined I could see out the window. My hand shook, pushing my cellphone tight to my ear as if that would keep anyone from knowing about my conversation.

"Honey," I said to my wife in a wavering voice. "There's just no way I can make it home."

"What do you mean, John?" she asked. "Don't you have a plane ticket to come home tomorrow?"

"Of course I do," I replied. "But, I just can't fly home tomorrow. I just can't."

"Did your meetings run long? Is there a crisis? What's going on?" Kathy was growing frustrated trying to understand what I was telling her.

"Look," I said finally. "I know this is stupid, but I just

can't get on the plane." I paused, then finally let the truth out. "I'm too scared."

If I had expected my wife to be empathetic to my cause I was sorely mistaken. It's not that my wife doesn't love me. I'm sure she loves me with all her heart. It's just that she's eminently practical.

"What do you mean?" She asked.

"I mean, I can't. I mean I can't even convince myself to go to the airport. I mean the flight isn't scheduled for another 14 hours and I'm already sweating and shaking like a leaf. I'm just really scared."

To her credit, my wife never belittled my fear. We talked for a few more minutes, most of which was spent by me trying to convince her that we could move to Baltimore and start a new life in that fine city. Somehow she couldn't see the logic in that point of view.

Finally she said, "Look honey, this is ridiculous. You have to come home sometime and there's no reason it shouldn't be tomorrow. Baltimore is a decent-sized city. Instead of flying home, why don't you buy a train ticket? I'm sure Amtrak goes from Baltimore to Chicago."

Of course! A train. That was a great idea. I've always liked trains. There's just something romantic about the clickety clack of the tracks and the sense that you're traveling just as people have for generations. It would be relaxing. Sure, it might take a bit longer, but trains go all over the country. I might never have to fly again.

So, the next morning I bought a train ticket—Baltimore to Philadelphia, then Philadelphia to Chicago. I got on the train and sat down in my seat.

# INTRODUCTION

"This is the way to travel," I thought. "I have lots of legroom, nice wide seats, and I can get up and walk around any time I want."

The trip to Philadelphia only took an hour and fifteen minutes. With three hours to kill in the city of brotherly love, I considered going out to see the Liberty Bell or some of the other sites. After thinking about it, though, I was afraid I wouldn't be able to make it back in time to board the train to Chicago, and I really didn't want to have to explain that to my wife.

Two and a half hours later I sat in my seat waiting to get going when a large man shuffled down the aisle and, wouldn't you know it, sat down in the seat right next to me. Now, I'm a large man myself, and when two large men sit next to each other on a train, there's an inevitable jockeying for space. It's not as bad as on a plane, but the issue remains. To make matters worse, this particular man had a peculiar odor—the kind one has when one hasn't bathed in recent memory. Suddenly a nice 18-hour (that's right, 18-hour!) train ride became an endurance contest for my olfactory system.

I decided to try to make the best of it. "At least I can get some decent sleep," I thought. I kicked back the chair, which went almost completely horizontal, turned my face to the window and dozed off.

While I did find it easier to sleep on the train than on a plane (after all, it's almost impossible to sleep when you're sure death is imminent), I still tossed and turned. At one point during the night I woke up from a bizarre dream about the ocean. To my foggy brain, I was convinced I could hear the surf even after I was conscious. I knew I was awake because my back hurt, my eyes were open, and I was looking at the dark landscape passing by outside the window. It was then I realized that whatever was making the sound of the surf was pressed against my shoulder. Then it snorted. Mr. Large-and-Smelly was snoring in my ear as he used my shoulder for his pillow.

Those were the longest 18 hours I had ever experienced. I finally arrived in Chicago exhausted, stinky, cranky, and determined to beat this stupid fear of flying once and for all.

## CONFIDENCE CRISIS

How about you? What keeps you from living confidently in this chaotic world? What fears do you struggle with? What worries, anxieties and concerns keep you up at night? God tells us 365 different times in Scripture to "Fear not." You might think that a promise made by the Creator of all things and repeated once for every day of the year would instantly set our hearts at ease. To be honest, that's not been my experience. Though, I did beat the fear of flying. Two years after my trip to Baltimore, I took a job that required me to travel internationally six to eight times a year. I never took a train from Australia to Chicago!

God can conquer fear. Confidence can be built. In this book we'll use some of my own experiences growing in confidence as a kind of case study, and dig deep into Scripture to see what God says about confidence and how to build it. We'll also get really practical about what you can do to be more confident in the midst of the chaos of this world.

## THE JOURNEY AHEAD

The book is laid out in four sections. In section one we'll discover the four requirements for confidence, why self-confidence is a dead end, and what to do instead. In section two, we'll see several ways God demonstrates his goodness to us and learn how to connect the dots between his goodness and our need for confidence. Section three will lift the curtain on God's greatness, showing us specific ways that his greatness can be applied to set us on rock solid ground. Finally, in section four we'll explore seven specific steps you can take to create your own personalized confidence plan.

Let's get started!

### SECTION 1
# THE FOUR REQUIREMENTS OF GOD-CONFIDENCE

Before we can grow in confidence, we need to understand what it actually is, and what prerequisites there may be to attaining it. We can get thrown off track before we've even begun if we don't understand the fundamental requirements for having confidence. In this section we'll start there and quickly see that conventional wisdom can't help us live confidently in a chaotic world.

## CHAPTER 1
# CONFIDENCE REQUIRES PERFECTION

Across the street from Centennial Olympic Park in Atlanta, Georgia, sits a weirdly modern building claiming to be a museum. In reality this building guards the mysteries of one of the most influential organizations in world history. Deep within the walls of this strange building, hidden within a rarely opened vault, lies the secret of the organization's power. It is rumored that only two men are aware of what is in the vault, and even then, each man knows only half of the truth so that it cannot be forced from either. I'm writing, of course, of the secret formula for Coca-Cola.

Secrets and mysteries fascinate us. Not to be outdone by Coke's secret formula, KFC developed its own origin story around the secret recipe for its fried chicken. McDonald's has closely guarded the ingredients in its "secret sauce" used on the Big Mac. Google has secret algorithms which guide its search engine. If a company could plumb their mysteries, it could be the number one hit every time someone searched for anything related to their industry.

There's a not-so-secret formula for confidence, as well. Once you understand it, the mysteries of confident living began to break open for anyone to utilize.

Shh. Look around. Is anyone listening? No? Okay. Here it is:

$$\text{CONFIDENCE} = \frac{\text{PERFORMANCE}}{\text{TIME}}$$

This formula indicates that the degree to which a person can be legitimately confident is directly related to their performance over a substantial period of time.

Let me give you an example. In university I was a jazz trumpet major. Anyone who has played trumpet knows that the most exciting and valued skill is to be able to play very high notes. These are the notes that audiences applaud for, and other musicians wonder at. The ability to hit these notes ensures that a trumpet player will get gigs. There's just something visceral and energizing about a really high screaming trumpet part.

The challenge for trumpet players everywhere is that in order to learn to play those notes, you have to go all in. It takes a lot of breath and, typically, a lot of volume to hit them. Learning to play high notes follows the same pattern as learning any skill. You try and fail. You try and fail. You try and partially succeed. So, you first have to try and miss, again and again. And when you miss those high notes, they're really loud and they just kind of splatter all over the wall. Everybody knows when you miss.

So let's imagine we're playing a concert and I have to

play a high E flat. That's a pretty high note for an average-to-good trumpet player. Imagine I've been working really hard and over time I've got to the point where I can hit the E flat 50% of the time in practice. How confident am I that I'm going to hit that note in the performance? Probably not too confident. Chances are 50/50 at best, the flip of a coin. Add in the pressure and nerves of the performance, it's probably even lower. But now imagine I hit it 99 times out of 100 in practice. In fact, I can hit the G above the E flat. I nail it again and again. Now, how confident am I? Much more, right? The secret to confidence is performance over time. How do you perform over a decent amount of time? That is the level of your confidence. Now, if you're truly going to be confident, you need to have very high, and very consistent, performance. To have perfect confidence, you need perfect performance over time. Otherwise, there's always room for doubt. Even if I hit that E flat 99 times out of 100, when the pressure is on and the audience is out there, there's still a little voice in my head saying, "What if this is the one time in a hundred that you miss?"

Confidence equals performance over time. In order to have perfect confidence, we need to have perfect performance.

## WHAT'S YOUR DEAL?

You probably aren't a trumpet player hoping to hit high notes. You may not struggle with a fear of flying. So, what's your deal? Everyone has at least one issue they struggle to feel confident about. You may hate trying to make small talk in a social situation. Maybe your blood runs cold if you have to speak in front of people. You may struggle with something more subtle. Perhaps you live with ongoing anxiety for the well-being of your children. You might be concerned about world events, the economy, or crime in your neighborhood. Or you might live under the shadow of impostor syndrome—the feeling that if people really knew you, they'd see that you aren't as good as people think. Some of the matters that sap our confidence are long-term challenges. Others are more seasonal. Financial pressures may weigh heavy on your heart right now. You may be in a season of life when your health or the health of your parents or loved ones is of great concern.

Before we move on, let's take a few minutes to identify some of the concerns you have that keep you from living confidently in this chaotic world. On the next page is a chart to help you. While certainly not an exhaustive list, many confidence-sappers can be identified in one of these categories.

Now, think back over the last several weeks. Have you performed perfectly in the area that concerns you? Yeah. Me neither. What are the other factors involved in the area you're concerned about? It may or may not be in your control, but unless it performs perfectly, your confidence will diminish. Your retirement account, the weather, the reaction of friends and loved ones, your body's response to illness and medication, whatever the issue is, chances are imperfect performance is the normal experience. Stretch that imperfection out over a lifetime and you can see why most of us struggle to live confidently in our chaotic world.

## MORE SELF-CONFIDENCE?

Self-confidence follows this same equation. You will be confident in yourself in whatever the situation is—whether it's making small talk at a party (which I hate) or it's public speaking, or it's getting on an airplane, or facing a job interview—your confidence in yourself will only rise to the level of your own performance in that area over time.

That's the bad news.

The good news is there's a better way, and you don't have to consistently raise your performance in order to raise your confidence. Because if that were the case, life would be a long, hard journey, a road of always trying to get better at everything. This is why self-confidence is a trap. In order to grow in self-confidence, you need to continually improve at whatever you're concerned about. So, I need to get better at communicating with my wife, better at motivating my employees, better at pleasing my boss, better at taking tests and writing papers, better at understanding the opposite sex (good luck with that one!), better at ... just about everything. Now that's a lot of pressure!

Thankfully, there's a better way, but it's not self-confidence. Self-confidence always dead ends in one of two ways. First, you may have low self-confidence, based on inconsistent performance. You hope you'll do better, you pray this is the time you come through, but you're often disappointed because you're not perfect. Every time you let yourself down, your confidence erodes just a little bit more. The other way self-confidence dead ends is in total arrogance. This happens when your confidence rises beyond the level

## ABILITY TO ACHIEVE

- Personal finances
- Keeping the house clean
- Meeting work or school goals
- Parenting skills
- Choosing a career

## SENSE OF IDENTITY

- Physical appearance
- Fitness
- Fashion sense
- Finding a spouse
- Having a child

## RELATIONSHIPS

- What others think
- Interpersonal communication
- Relational conflict
- Sex life

## EVENTS

- Crime, war, and violence
- Economy and job security
- Finding a new job
- Hunger and famine
- Pandemic

## WELLBEING OF OTHERS

- Loved one's health
- Pet's health
- Child's ability to succeed

## ABILITY TO FUNCTION

- Aging
- Personal physical health
- Personal mental health
- Addiction
- Financial health

of your performance. Essentially, your confidence is based on a lie. In the end, self-confidence isn't actually confidence at all. It's self hope. I hope I can do this. If I try hard enough, if I grit my teeth, if I pray the right prayers and say the magic words, I'll nail it this time.

Self-confidence always ends up in either arrogance or insecurity. Let me give you an example. The year 2015 was special for Cam Newton, the quarterback for the Carolina Panthers. From the time he came into the National Football League he was on a very steep, upward trajectory. In terms of skill, ability, and performance, he was the total package. Then, in 2015 he led his team to a perfect season. Yep, perfect. Undefeated. Sixteen regular season wins and zero losses. They were perfect in their two playoff games as well. Cam was the man. He was on fire. He was winning and winning and winning, and poised to do something no other quarterback in NFL history had ever done: Lead his team to a 16-win regular season and finish as world champions.

Cam was known for his confidence. Whenever he would score, he would mime the action of ripping his shirt open like Superman to reveal the letter "S" on his chest. Going into Super Bowl 50 against the Denver Broncos, Cam was ready. Almost everybody said he was going to lead his team to victory. It was going to be amazing.

Then something totally unexpected happened. Cam Newton only completed 44% of his passes. He turned the ball over to the other team three times, throwing an interception and fumbling the ball twice. His second fumble sealed the deal. The mighty Carolina Panthers, undefeated in every game of the season—18 straight games, lost.

Was Cam Newton confident? Absolutely. Did his confidence pay off? Absolutely not. Did he have a great track record to look back on? Absolutely. Was it a perfect track record? Of course not. In the end, his super-high self-confidence was misplaced and led to his team's defeat. That's always the case with self-confidence. It's how self-confidence works. It will eventually lead you to either arrogance or insecurity.

## NOT THE ANSWER

Trying to achieve more self-confidence is not the answer you're looking for. Let me give you three reasons why pursuing self-confidence is a dead end.

First, in order to be perfectly self-confident, we need to know everything perfectly. There can be no surprises. But, our knowledge is insufficient. We do not know enough. Cam Newton did not know what the Denver Broncos defense was going to throw at him. If he had known it, he would have prepared differently, but our knowledge is incomplete. We just don't know everything. Because our knowledge is insufficient, we can't be perfectly confident. There will always be doubt.

Second, our performance is inconsistent. We just aren't perfect. We simply don't do everything exactly right every single time. Since our performance is inconsistent, our self-confidence will be inconsistent. Or, it will be based on a lie and turn into arrogance. In other words, instead of having true self-confidence, we'll just pretend that we're better than we really are.

Third, our power is insufficient. We are not powerful

enough to ensure perfect performance. When Cam Newton got to the second quarter of Superbowl 50 he knew changes needed to be made in order to defeat the Denver Broncos. What they had planned wasn't working. However, he didn't have the power to do what was necessary. He couldn't change the way his teammates were thinking. He couldn't give them more understanding, more energy, more strength. He couldn't ensure that he made all the right decisions for the rest of the game. He wasn't capable of throwing all the right passes. He wasn't even powerful enough to hold on to the ball to avoid the two fumbles he made. Please understand, my point isn't to pick on Cam Newton. I'm sure he's a wonderful person. His experience in Super Bowl 50 is simply a perfect example of the fact that we can never have enough-self confidence to ensure success and that pursuing self-confidence is, in itself, a dead end. Our power is insufficient. Because there are times when we fail, if we are emotionally honest, we cannot be perfectly confident in ourselves.

## A BETTER WAY

Self-confidence says, "I can do it" and relies on my abilities and performance. However, Scripture never says to have more self-confidence. There's no verse that says, "have more self-confidence and be more confident in yourself. Buck up, Buckaroo! You can do it." That's not the message of the Bible. Rather than exhorting us to have more confidence in ourselves, Scripture encourages us to have confidence in God. Instead of saying, "I can do it," God-confidence says, "Whether or not I can do it, God will be with me."

Here's how the prophet Jeremiah explains it in the Old Testament.

> *Thus says the LORD: "Cursed is the man who trusts in man and makes flesh his strength, whose heart turns away from the LORD. He is like a shrub in the desert, and shall not see any good come. He shall dwell in the parched places of the wilderness, in an uninhabited salt land. (Jeremiah 17:5-6)*

Cursed is the one who trusts in man, in humans? That's pretty intense. Why does Jeremiah say they are cursed? Because they're always going to have doubt. Their life will be a series of peaks and valleys based on whether they and others come through or not. When their performance is good, they'll be happy and confident. When their performance is bad, they'll be discouraged and insecure. Up, down, up, down, up, down. In reality, trusting in yourself—honest self-confidence—results in less confidence, because you're always unsure of the result. That's no way to live.

CHAPTER 2

# CONFIDENCE REQUIRES DISCERNMENT

How do you feel when you don't feel confident? Nervous? Worried? Concerned? Frustrated?

I'd like to suggest that there are basically only four emotions. We use lots of different English words for them, sometimes trying to pretend we don't really feel what we are really feeling. But in the end, we have four basic choices. We can be glad—happy, joyful, chipper, content, excited. We can be mad—angry, frustrated, annoyed, vexed. We can be sad—melancholy, wistful, somber, blue, down. Or we can be scared—anxious, afraid, concerned, nervous, insecure. Whatever words we use, they are basically synonyms for one of the four basic emotions: glad, sad, mad, or scared. Christians especially try to mask our emotions. We're not mad; we're frustrated. I'm not scared; I'm just concerned. In the long run, this is simply emotional dishonesty and only serves to confuse the issue. To grow in confidence we need to be honest with how we feel. If we aren't feeling confident (a subset of glad) we're probably feeling scared.

## GOOD EMOTIONS, BAD EMOTIONS?

Let's pause a minute to take our emotional temperature. Close your eyes. Take a deep breath. Pay attention to your feelings. Are you perfectly content, relaxed, confident, and at ease? If not, then there is likely some aspect of fear in your life. The opposite of confidence is fear. I might say I'm concerned; I'm bothered; I am uneasy; or I'm troubled, but these are all just different ways of saying I'm scared. So if you're scared, the question is, why are you scared? The emotion itself is neither good nor bad.

All four emotions are gifts from God and each one serves a purpose in our lives. The emotion itself is neutral; it's just a feeling. Happiness is neither good nor bad. You can be happy for good reasons. Perhaps you are celebrating an anniversary, or you just received a promotion at work. Those are good reasons to be happy. You can also be happy for bad reasons. Maybe you just told off your roommate and it made you feel good, or someone you don't like at work just got fired. Those aren't very good reasons to be happy. You may be sad because your dog died (a good reason to be sad). Or you may be sad because your husband doesn't read your mind and instinctively know you wish he'd take you out for dinner tonight (a selfish reason to be sad)[1]. There is nothing inherently good or bad about emotions, they are simply the way we feel at any given time. Glad, sad, mad, scared.

Recently I was quite angry with a colleague. Several days went by before I could approach him about the issue and, to be honest, the anger really grew during that time. I was making up all kinds of terrible things about him and how I was going to ensure that Justice (with a capital J) was served. When we did sit down and discuss it, I was surprised to find that he was just as angry at me as I was at him. In my mind I was the white knight in this situation and he was in allegiance with the devil. But, the more we talked about it, the more I saw his side of what had happened. And he understood more of what I had experienced. In actual fact, once we were able to work through the feelings, we realized that we had both screwed up. At the same time, neither one of us had screwed up as intentionally and malevolently as the other had imagined.

Emotions are neutral, neither good nor bad in themselves. However, how we feel may be based on ideas that aren't true. We may need to inform our feelings, to educate them. We can make sure they are based on reality and not just a partial understanding of the truth. Once we get all the facts, our feelings may, and possibly should, change. A feeling is just a feeling. Whether you're mad, sad, glad, or scared, there is nothing wrong with that feeling. Just take the time to make sure it's based in reality.[2] Emotions are just emotions. It's good to feel our feelings, whatever they are. Then we can diagnose where the emotions are coming from. If I'm scared (afraid, lacking in confidence) why is that?

Several years ago my friend and coworker Mario and I were attending a meeting in downtown Chicago. As the morning went on, I started to feel sick. For the last couple of days I'd had this weird metallic taste in my mouth and now I was getting lightheaded and weak.

Once the meeting was over and my friend started driving us back to our office, I said, "Mario, I think you need to drive me to the hospital." Keeping his eyes on the road Mario asked, "Oh, what's going on?"

"Well," I said, "I can't feel the left side of my face and I can't close my left eye. There's something wrong here."

"All right. Which hospital would you like me to go to?" he asked, like this was something that happened all the time. (Later Mario told me that though he seemed totally cool on the outside, he was trying to keep his voice from shaking because he was so freaked out on the inside.)

Once we got to the emergency room, they quickly put me in a bed and took my vitals. As I lay there waiting to see a doctor my mind started to work the problem. Soon I realized what the issue was. Years ago I received a mercury filling in one of my teeth. Over the years, the mercury had leached into my bloodstream and I was now going to die of mercury poisoning. It was the only answer.

Soon enough the doctor came in to see me. He looked at my chart. He looked in my mouth. He poked me a bunch of times in the face. "Do you feel this?" he asked each time. He ordered some blood tests. He sent me for a CT scan. Then I waited. Each moment that passed I became more convinced I would see Jesus face-to-face before the day was over. I had mixed feelings about that.

Finally, "Doctor Pokey" came back. "I'm pretty sure I know what's wrong with you." (Pretty sure? I'm absolutely sure I'm dying of mercury poisoning.) He said, "You have Bell's palsy. It's a disease without a known cause and without a real cure. Our best guess is that it's a virus that attacks the nerve that runs from your spinal cord, under your ear and controls the entire side of your face. We'll give you an antiviral and some steroids on the off-chance that they'll help, but most people get better within six to nine months."

Oh. So, I wasn't dying. I was just drooping. Over the next few hours I would lose total control of the left half of my face. I had to be careful when I ate. I had to take special care of my left eye since it wouldn't blink on its own and never completely closed. But, I didn't have mercury poisoning. I wasn't going to die, at least not yet.

As I'm writing this, two and a half years have passed. I have regained control over most of that side of my face. A person has to look carefully to tell that my smile is still kind of crooked. If I'm tired you might hear me slur some words. At this point, it's just a nuisance. But imagine if the doctors had taken my diagnosis as accurate and said, "Yeah, if that's what it is, we better treat you for mercury poisoning."

Well, there's no cure for mercury poisoning. The treatment would have included drilling out all of my fillings and replacing them, which by itself gives me the cold sweats. I would have been put on a long-term intravenous therapy designed to help the organs get rid of the mercury. This therapy can cause convulsions, seizures, respiratory failure, anemia, blood infections, kidney damage, liver failure, and brain damage. No thanks.

In medicine, the right diagnosis is everything. A lot of harm, up to, and including, death, can be done by acting on an incorrect diagnosis. The same is true in every area of life. Our diagnosis of any problem, whether it's a health issue, a relational problem, a marketing challenge, or a sports competition, determines our "treatment" or our actions. If our diagnosis is incorrect, our actions will be ineffective at best and harmful at worst. For this reason, discernment is needed as we look at confidence and its opposite, fear. Correctly diagnosing the cause of our lack of confidence and our fear is necessary in order to treat it correctly.

## A STUDY IN CONTRASTS

Ahaz, King of Judah, has a problem. Eleven generations after the great King Solomon, he lacks all the wisdom of his ancestor, as well as Solomon's commitment to the Lord. He was not a good King. Right now Ahaz is facing a war in which he is greatly outnumbered. Two kingdoms, each of which are larger than his, have joined forces to come against him.

What is Ahaz doing? He's freaking out. The Bible describes it this way.

> *When the house of David was told, "Syria is in league with Ephraim," the heart of Ahaz and the heart of his people shook as the trees of the forest shake before the wind. (Isaiah 7:2)*

They are shaking. That's how scared they are, and for good reason. They were outnumbered. They were being attacked by two nations, but listen to what God says to Ahaz through the prophet Isaiah.

> *"Be careful, be quiet, do not fear, and do not let your heart be faint because of these two smoldering stumps of firebrands ... If you are not firm in faith, you will not be firm at all.'" (Isaiah 7:4, 9)*

## CONFIDENCE REQUIRES DISCERNMENT

God says, "Don't worry; don't be afraid." Then he says, "If you aren't strong in your faith, you aren't strong at all." In other words, the important thing here is Ahaz's faith. Sure, with his physical eyes Ahaz can only see the multitude of men coming to attack him. But God says, "There's a larger reality at work here. I'm going to save you. Trust me." But Ahaz won't. He refuses to see that faith is the real challenge he faces. Ahaz misdiagnosed the situation. He thinks he's in danger because these armies are coming out to attack him and he's out-gunned. In reality, he's in danger because he has no faith. Lack of faith leads to fear. The problem isn't his earthly view of the chaotic situation. He fully understands that reality. The problem is his heavenly view of the conquering God. This, in spite of the fact that God had already delivered Ahaz's people from similar situations in previous generations. God's track record was there for him to see.

Faith is the core of everything in the Christian life, but especially the core of confidence. Now, let's fast forward one generation to Ahaz's son, Hezekiah. A very similar situation occurs. This time it's the king of Assyria, the world power at the time, who comes to attack. The Assyrians are clever. The king sends messengers to Hezekiah with these instructions:

> *"Thus shall you speak to Hezekiah king of Judah: 'Do not let your God in whom you trust deceive you by promising that Jerusalem will not be given into the hand of the king of Assyria. Behold, you have heard what the kings of Assyria have done to all lands, devoting them to*

> destruction. And shall you be delivered?
> (2 Kings 19:10-11)

Before he attacks Judah's capital with his armies, he attacks their hope with his words. This pagan king understands better than Ahaz did that the primary battle is the battle for faith, for belief.

Hezekiah's response is profoundly different from his father's. Rather than shaking like a leaf, Hezekiah takes the declaration of war from the king of Assyria into the temple, spreads it out before the Lord, and prays. Here's what he says.

> *Truly, O LORD, the kings of Assyria have laid waste the nations and their lands ... So now, O LORD our God, save us, please, from his hand, that all the kingdoms of the earth may know that you, O LORD, are God alone."*
> (2 Kings 19:17, 19)

Hezekiah says to God, "Look, they're right. They're stronger than us. They've conquered all these other kings and kingdoms. But Lord, we know that you are God of all the kingdoms of the earth." Look at the purpose he gives for wanting God to save them. "That the earth may know that you, O LORD, are God alone." He sees the big picture. This isn't just a spat between two kingdoms. God's reputation is on the line here. Hezekiah has faith that God can do something, wants to do something about it. God responds through the prophet Isaiah, saying, "I will defend this city to save it, for my own sake and for the sake of my servant

David." (2 Kings 19:34) The next morning Hezekiah and his people wake up to find that the Assyrian army has retreated, leaving behind 180,000 dead brothers in arms. Wow.

So, what was the difference between Ahaz and Hezekiah, his son? How was it that Hezekiah could see the possibilities of what God could do, even in the face of overwhelming physical evidence to the contrary? The secret is found in the book of 2 Kings. Scripture says Hezekiah "trusted in the LORD, the God of Israel, so that there was none like him among all the kings of Judah after him, nor among those who were before him." (2 Kings 18:5) The difference was faith, trust, belief. Where Ahaz couldn't imagine what God was capable of because he didn't have faith, his son Hezekiah did because he cultivated faith in God throughout his life.

Life is hard. Chaos happens. Do we want to face it like Ahaz or like Hezekiah? How we handle life's difficulties depends entirely on how we diagnose the problem. Is the problem you face rooted in your circumstances? Is it a health problem, a financial problem, a relational problem? Or is the problem rooted in your heart? Is it primarily a faith problem? I don't want to suggest for a minute that your circumstances aren't real and difficult. Hezekiah's circumstances were dire indeed. It's easy for us to forget how serious they were because we know the end of the story, but put yourself in his shoes. What must it have been like to have heard the news of the Assyrians conquering all the nations around you over the years and suddenly find that their army has you surrounded? How must he have felt, standing on the walls of the city, looking out over the hundreds of thousands of well-trained, well-armed soldiers, fresh from their latest conquest, eager for your blood? It was a very real problem, but the deeper issue was his faith.

You and I will face difficult circumstances again and again. Sometimes it seems we just make it through one crisis to find ourselves facing another. However dire the circumstances, however difficult our situation, the key question is whether we will face it in faith or in fear. We really can live confidently, even in the midst of horrible circumstances, by growing in faith. Faith is just another word for God-confidence.

## DISCERNING BETWEEN FEAR AND CONCERN

Earlier we said that there are really only four emotions: glad, sad, mad, and scared. We can use all types of synonyms for them, but they all come back to one of those four. One of the words we sometimes use to mask the fact that we are scared is "concern." I'm not worried; I'm not afraid; I'm just concerned. There is a legitimate difference between fear and concern, though the line can sometimes be very thin. I may be concerned that my daughter is struggling in science class. This concern can lead me to pay closer attention to her homework, keep tabs on her test scores, and regularly encourage her to do her best. This is a healthy concern. I'm not freaking out. I haven't turned into a helicopter parent, micromanaging every aspect of my daughter's life. I'm not catastrophizing the issue, believing if she gets a poor grade in 5th grade science she'll never get into a good college, never find a decent career, and end up living on the street. No, I'm just concerned and that concern has led me to take some action.

On the other hand, this same concern may easily slip into fear. A few low test scores and suddenly I'm convinced it's the end of the world. So here's the question, is it fear or is it concern? How can I tell the difference? There is legitimate concern that doesn't morph into fear. When do I know I've crossed the line? The secret to determining if concern has slipped into fear is to ask yourself, "Who bears ultimate responsibility for the result?"

As I lay in the hospital bed, convinced that I was suffering from mercury poisoning I had allowed healthy concern to grow into unhealthy fear. Why? Because I believed the ultimate responsibility for fixing it lay in human hands. Of course, I believed God could heal and might possibly intervene, but at the most foundational level I didn't believe he would. I believed that my health rested in the hands of the doctors to treat me appropriately. I couldn't see any future scenario in which I might not be healed and yet life could be good, so I was afraid.

The apostle Paul assures us in Romans 8:28 that God works all things together for good, for those who are called according to his purpose. If what Paul said is true, then instead of being afraid I could have faced that situation with faith—with God-confidence.

Let's say that I did have mercury poisoning. Let's imagine that the doctors weren't able to really address it. The effects of the poisoning stayed with me for the rest of my life. According to Paul, God would ensure that someday I'd be able to look back on it and actually be thankful for it. I could trust that God was working all things—even the poison, the pain, and the hardship of living with its after effects—together for good because I'm called according to his purpose.

Fear bears the weight of personal responsibility. Concern recognizes the ultimate responsibility is God's. Of course that doesn't mean that we can be stupid or lazy. There are actions that we can, and should, take in faith. If you lose your job, you should probably look for a new one. If you're sick, you should probably go to a doctor. Common sense comes into play here. Assuming you are faithful to do the responsible thing, then who are you trusting to bear the burden? Is your faith in your own work and actions, or is it in God's care and faithfulness?

## DISCERNING THE CAUSE

Have you ever been going throughout your day and suddenly asked yourself, "Why do I feel so sad all of a sudden?" Or, "Why am I so angry right now?" Perhaps you've been debating something with a friend and without warning you find your voice rising, your fists clenching, and your blood boiling. "Whoa, where did that come from?" you wonder. Emotions have a way of sneaking up on us. We don't always know at a conscious level why we feel the way we do. Sometimes it takes some investigation. If we are to grow in God-confidence, understanding the cause of our emotion is vital. We can't move from fear, worry, concern, and nervousness to confidence and faith until we understand where we're starting from.

An emotion can be rooted in one of four causes. They might be based on our intellect. Something in our knowledge, information, or belief system can trigger our feelings. When our emotions are based on our intellect, the health of our feelings is directly tied to the veracity of the knowledge, information, or beliefs we hold. I may be angry because I just saw a father scream at his young son. Based on the information I observed, I feel protective of the child and angry at the father. What if, unbeknownst to me, the father was yelling at his son because his son was about to run out into the street and be hit by an oncoming car? Would receiving that additional information change how I feel? Of course. Instead of being angry at the father, I would be glad that the son was saved from harm. Sometimes poor or incomplete information means our emotions aren't anchored in reality.

Feelings might arise from physical causes. Anxiety (another name for fear) can be the result of imbalances in brain chemistry. Neurotransmitters like serotonin, dopamine, and others are linked to mood and anxiety disorders.

In general I believe Christians have been slow to understand issues involving mental health. We have been too quick to assume that emotions are always within our conscious control and that "bad emotions" are simply the result of sin or a lack of faith. We've already made clear that there are no "bad emotions." There are only emotions. We simply feel the way we feel. Those feelings may be based on imperfect information, in which case we can inform and educate them, but the emotions themselves are neither good nor bad. This is why discernment is needed when it comes to diagnosing the cause of our feelings. It's possible that anxiety is a result of lack of faith. In that case additional information and practice (more on this later) can help move a person from anxiety to confidence. However, it's also true that anxiety may be rooted in physical disease. When that's the case, then treating the physical issue underlying the emotional ones is the right move.

The summer after my freshman year of college, I joined a missionary team in Europe for three months. Shortly after I arrived I fell down a mountain (don't ask, it's a long story) and busted my knee wide open. When the team reached me, no one said, "John, you need to confess your sin so God will heal your knee." None of them told me, "You just need to increase your faith, John, and this problem will go away." No, of course not. They hiked me into the van and rushed me to the hospital for immediate surgery. And I'm glad they did.

If we don't say those kinds of things when someone faces a physical health problem, then why do we say them when someone struggles with a mental health problem? Why is it fine to take medicine for a sinus infection, but suspect to take medicine to normalize your brain chemistry? If you've struggled with anxiety (fear) or depression (sadness) over a period of time, don't assume it's a character defect or a sin. It might be, but there may be other issues at play. Go see a professional. Talk to your doctor. Those are totally legitimate courses of action.

Of course it's also possible that your feelings do have spiritual causes. It could be that you're hiding sin. It could be that you have an idol in your heart. It could be that the enemy is attacking you and you're facing spiritual warfare. It could be that spiritual, physical, and intellectual causes are working together. This is why discernment is needed.

The final potential cause of emotions is volitional. Your volition is your will. It's what primarily motivates your choices and decisions. I want to do something, or I don't. Those choices naturally lead to certain feelings.

Just last weekend I had an experience where my feelings were rooted in my volition. I needed to make some choices about where to focus my ministry over the next eight months. I had the opportunity to preach quite a bit more than normal, or I could take the opportunity to work with some small groups and ministry teams behind the scenes. I really love to preach. It's one of my favorite activities, and I don't get to do it nearly as often as I would like. And yet ... it really seemed as if God was inviting me to do this other work behind the scenes. You know what? I was mad. In fact, I was so cranky in church this past Sunday that I left early. (Shh. Please don't tell anyone.) I didn't even understand why I was mad until I talked it through with my wife and daughter. They helped me see that I was choosing to be angry at God and others rather than choosing to submit to what he was calling me to. My emotions were rising from my will.

In this case, volitional and spiritual causes worked together in a negative fashion, but it doesn't always happen that way. Sometimes volitional causes are positive. Turning off the television in order to read Scripture may make you feel good about your choice to invest in your relationship with God. You may feel glad you chose to shop at the second hand store and paid a quarter of what you would at a brand name outlet. All four emotions can proceed from any of the four causes: intellectual, physical, spiritual, or volitional.

## DIAGNOSTIC QUESTIONS

Two diagnostic questions can help us discern what is going on with our emotions when we struggle with confidence. First, who bears responsibility? Second, how long has the fear lasted? Fear, just like the other three emotions, is a gift from God. The purpose of fear is to motivate action in order to get us out of harm's way.

Let's say you're walking alongside a set of train tracks on your way to grandmother's house. As you round a bend in the tracks the serenity of your walk is pierced by a loud whistle. Looking up, you're startled to see a great locomotive bearing down on you at 50 miles per hour. Whoa! Your heart starts beating faster; your adrenaline spikes. You suddenly have supernatural speed. You scramble off the train tracks and roll down the embankment just as the train roars through the space you inhabited only a second before. Fear motivated you to do something, to change something, to get out of harm's way. That's God's good purpose for fear in our lives. However, you can't carry that kind of fear for very long.

Soldiers living in a war zone live in a kind of high octane environment for extended periods of time. Often it's super unhealthy. They come back struggling with nightmares, anxiety, and post-traumatic stress disorder. If you're feeling fear on an ongoing basis, that's probably a sign that there's something unhealthy going on behind the scenes.

Start by asking some questions. "Who's really responsible for this? Is there something I'm trying to avoid? What's the oncoming train I'm trying to jump away from?" Often we struggle with worry or low confidence, but we can't quite pinpoint what we're afraid of. We just experience this kind of generalized anxiety and don't know why. If we can isolate the cause, we can work on it. Knowing I'm afraid because a train is going to hit me a split second from now is easy, right? But discerning that my fear is the result of having a type "A" boss who reminds me of my emotionally unstable dad? That's harder to diagnose. Fortunately, God has provided people to help us as we navigate the process. Open up to a small group of trusted friends, a mentor, or a pastor. If they aren't helpful, see a professional counselor. That's what they're there for. Professionals are trained in asking the right kinds of questions to diagnose what's really going on.

## CHAPTER 3
# CONFIDENCE REQUIRES FEAR

When I was in elementary school we owned a Saint Bernard. One winter day I was lying on the couch in the living room while my family ate dinner in the dining room. I hadn't been feeling well and had developed a fever and didn't feel up to eating. As I lay there, Fritz-the-Saint-Bernard decided that my head would make an interesting chew toy. As he wrapped his jaws around my face and bit down I screamed down his throat hoping my family could hear me and come to the rescue. I still have the scars on the top of my head from his canines.

Years later Kathy, my girlfriend and future wife, introduced me to another dog. Kathy's parents owned a very large, very slobbery Great Dane. His name was Napoleon. My future in-laws were the kind of dog owners who would tell a visitor, "Oh, isn't that cute? She must like you" as the dog barked at you, put his front paws up on your shoulders, and looked in your eye as if to say, "I don't like you. Why don't you just run along home now with your tail between your legs?" Now, I actually like dogs. But, my earlier experience with Fritz-the-face-eating-Saint-Bernard had given me a deep respect for their ability to disobey their owners and for the sharpness of their teeth. I would spend the entire visit with my girlfriend's parents with my hands jammed in my pockets out of fear that Napoleon would hiccup and accidentally sever them from my arms. I dreaded going to Kathy's parents' house and having to face Napoleon.

Confidence requires fear. At first blush this seems entirely illogical. Aren't confidence and fear opposites? Well, yes and no. There are a couple of definitions for fear in the dictionary. One is, "an unpleasant, often strong emotion caused by anticipation or awareness of danger." This is what we normally think of when we think of fear. However, fear can also be defined as, "profound reverence and awe especially toward God." When the Bible talks about fear, it has this idea of reverence or great respect. Fear is reverence to the ultimate degree.

Think about how immensely powerful God is. He created the universe; he breathed life into humanity; he controls the orbits of the largest planets and the movements of the smallest quarks. He's omnipotent, all powerful. He can do anything that is an appropriate use of his power. Now picture the power of a thunderstorm. I'm not talking about just any kind of ordinary storm, I want you to imagine a good 'ole Midwestern, tornado-producing thunderstorm that shoots great bolts of lightning to the ground. The booming reverberation of its thunderclaps sends dogs in six counties running for cover underneath the nearest porch. The winds it produces threaten to blow semi-trucks into ditches. Roadside billboards bow to its greatness.

Which is more powerful, God or the thunderstorm? Which commands more reverence? It's easy to say that God is more powerful than the strongest thunderstorm, but in real life, it may be the storm that commands more reverence. What we reverence changes us. It asserts a level of control over our thoughts, actions, and feelings. Very few of us would continue our golf game when overtaken by a violent thunderstorm. No, after considering the options, we would seek shelter, delaying our plans, staying away from windows, and waiting for the weather to change. We might start counting the seconds between flashes of lightning and cracks of thunder trying to discern how close the storm is and whether it's moving our way. It's possible we could feel some apprehension about what kind of damage this storm could do. Our appreciation, or reverence, for the power of the thunderstorm alters our thoughts, feelings, and actions.

In the Bible, the book of 1 Samuel, chapter 17 tells us the story of David and Goliath. The people of Israel were at war against the Philistines. Each army was camped opposite the other on either side of a large valley. Every morning Goliath, a Philistine giant, would come to the front line and yell to the Israelite army, taunting them and demanding that one of them come out to fight him. Verse 24 records the response of Israel's army. *All the men of Israel, when they saw the man, fled from him and were much afraid. (1 Samuel 17:24)* When David heard the giant mocking the army of Israel, he had a different response. *David said to the men who stood by him, "Who is this uncircumcised Philistine, that he should defy the armies of the living God?" (1 Samuel 17:26)* The men of Israel feared, or revered, the power of the Philistine giant. David understood the danger. He wasn't necessarily unafraid, but he had greater reverence for the power of God than the power of Goliath. When the Bible tells us to fear the Lord it means that we should revere him more than we revere anything or anyone else. Because what we revere controls us. Their fear of Goliath sent the Israelite army running away from him as fast as their sandaled feet would take them. David's fear of God sent him running towards the giant with faith in his heart and a stone in his sling.

> *Then David said to the Philistine, "You come to me with a sword and with a spear and with a javelin, but I come to you in the name of the LORD of hosts, the God of the armies of Israel, whom you have defied. This day the LORD will deliver you into my hand, and I will strike you down and cut off your head. And I will give the dead bodies of the host of the Philistines this day to the birds of the air and to the wild beasts of the earth, that all the earth may know that there is a God in Israel, and that all this assembly may know that the LORD saves not with sword and spear. For the battle is the LORD's, and he will give you into our hand." When the Philistine arose and came and drew near to meet David, David ran quickly toward the battle line to meet the Philistine. And David put his hand in his bag and took out a stone and slung it and struck the Philistine on his forehead. The stone sank into his forehead, and he fell on his face to the ground. So David prevailed over the Philistine with a sling and with a stone, and struck the Philistine and*

*killed him. There was no sword in the hand of David.
(1 Samuel 17:26, 45-50)*

Notice the last sentence of the story. There was no sword in the hand of David. The author is making the point that David didn't win the battle with superior weapons, superior strength, or superior strategy. In fact, in one sense David didn't win the battle at all. No, God won the battle through David's faith. Because David revered God's power more than Goliath's power, his thoughts, feelings, and actions were influenced by God and not the giant. On the other hand, the Israelite army's thoughts, feelings, and actions were controlled by their reverence for the power of Goliath.

When I was a kid I was afraid of thunderstorms. That's normal for kids, because thunderstorms are big and loud, and the lightning happens all of a sudden and is mysterious and can't be anticipated. I had seen the damage lightning could do to trees and knew the damage it could do to me. It's normal, and maybe even healthy, for a kid to have some fear of thunderstorms. An intelligent understanding of the capacity for damage that thunderstorms bring leads to a healthy fear of them.

For me, though, that fear never went away as I grew up. As a young adult, I would run in the rain from my apartment to my car, afraid to carry my keys because I might get struck by lightning. At home, I would sit as far away from the windows as possible so if lightning struck I wouldn't be in its path. Biblical fear is the belief in the power of a thing or person. I believed in the power of the thunderstorm to hurt me, but did I believe in the power of God to keep me safe? No, it was the thunderstorm, not God, controlling my thoughts, feelings, and actions. Clearly my fear of (reverence for) thunderstorms was greater than my fear of (reverence for) God.

When the Bible says, "Fear the Lord," it is telling us that our reverence for the Lord is to be higher than our fear of anything else. In Joshua 1:9 God tells Joshua to be strong and courageous. "I will go with you into the Promised Land. We're gonna take this. Don't be afraid of the Amalekites and the Ammorites and the Hittites and the Jebusites and the parasites and the other 'ites,' because I'm with you." Fear God most. Revere him more than anything else. Don't let other things influence you, controlling your thoughts, emotions, and actions. Only allow God to have that power in your life.

It took me a long time before I really believed God is bigger than the thunderstorms, but now, I love them. I enjoy watching them out the window. I wonder at the power they contain and how miniscule that is compared to God's power. My daughter and I make a party of it, popping popcorn and drinking tea. You can conquer whatever fear controls your actions, thoughts, and feelings, too.

Both faith and fear need an object. Our faith must be in something. I have faith in the chair I'm sitting in to hold me up. I have faith in my car, that it will start in the morning so I can drive to work. Faith needs an object. You can't just have faith generically. I've heard some very famous people say we just need to have faith in faith, as if faith itself does the work. But, that doesn't make any sense. It's like circular logic. Another word for faith is trust. You would never say,

"I have trust in trust." No, trust and faith need objects. What or who do you put your trust in? Do you trust in your spouse, your job, the economy, the government, or God? In the same way, we must ask ourselves, "What do we put our faith in?" Do we have faith in God or do we actually have more faith in other things? Faith needs an object.

Fear also needs an object. I'm afraid of some thing. I'm aware that some people struggle with something called generalized anxiety disorder. This is when you are anxious (another word for fear) about a lot of things all the time. You can't really pinpoint what exactly is causing it, and it just follows you around like an emotional case of tinnitus. But, for most of us, most of the time there is a specific cause or set of causes for our fear. What is it? If you can name it, you can figure out how to fear God more.

Let's approach it another way. Faith needs an object. Our faith is in something. Fear needs an object. Our fear is of something. Love also needs an object. It's an action verb. I may love pizza, paddle boating, or Snickers, but my love must have an object. Now, let's imagine that you're married. You have a spouse, but let's imagine that the object of your love is not, in fact, your spouse. Instead, you've decided that you love Mitch or Michelle more than you love your spouse. You're having an affair. We would call that adultery, right?

Now imagine that you have faith in God, but there is something that attracts your faith more than your faith in God. We call that idolatry. When my faith that the thunderstorm can hurt me is greater than my faith that God will keep me safe, I've made thunderstorms an idol. It's the thunderstorm that's controlling me. If my belief in the power of my mean boss to promote or demote me is stronger than my belief in God to control my future, I've made my boss an idol. I'm allowing his actions, words, and attitudes to control my thoughts, emotions, and actions.

## FEAR AND FEAR NOT

Moses had led the people of Israel out of Egypt. They had all witnessed the mighty plagues that God had brought on Pharaoh and the Egyptians. The path God had the Israelites take led them smack dab up against the Red Sea. With Pharaoh's army behind them and the Red Sea in front of them, they were freaking out pretty good.

> *They said to Moses, "Is it because there are no graves in Egypt that you have taken us away to die in the wilderness? What have you done to us in bringing us out of Egypt? Is not this what we said to you in Egypt: 'Leave us alone that we may serve the Egyptians'? For it would have been better for us to serve the Egyptians than to die in the wilderness." (Exodus 14:11-12)*

Before we get too critical of the Israelites, let's remember that for generations they had known nothing but slavery. There was no way for them to "get ahead," no way from them to prosper, the best they could do is keep their heads down, try not to make waves, and avoid getting whipped. So when they see the Egyptians coming after them, all they can think of is how ticked their masters must be and how much pain they're going to apply to their runaway slaves.

## CONFIDENCE REQUIRES FEAR

*And Moses said to the people, "Fear not, stand firm, and see the salvation of the LORD, which he will work for you today. For the Egyptians whom you see today, you shall never see again. The LORD will fight for you, and you have only to be silent." (Exodus 14:13-14)*

Excuse me, Moses, but do you see what the rest of us see? Are you sure the LORD is really speaking to you and you aren't imagining things?

Fear not.

What happens? God rescues them. They go through the sea on dry land. The water stacks up on either side of them like two giant walls.. The Egyptians come in after them. The sea crashes down over the Egyptians. Since the Egyptians never took Red Cross swimming lessons, they are utterly destroyed. Wow. Fear not, indeed.

Israel saw the great power that the LORD used against the Egyptians, so the people feared the LORD, and they believed in the LORD and in his servant Moses. (Exodus 14:31)

This is a great example of how the fear of the LORD works. In the first part of Exodus 14, the people of Israel are very afraid of the Egyptians and what they will do if they catch their former slaves. God tells them to stop it, to fear not. Why? Because there's Someone bigger in town than the Egyptians, and if they're busy fearing the Egyptians—allowing them to control how they think, feel, and act—then they aren't fearing the LORD.

At the end of Exodus 14, the Bible says that they now fear the LORD, and that's a good thing. Why is it good?

Because they are no longer allowing something or someone smaller to control them. Instead, they are responding to the one who is greater than everything and truly deserves their reverence and worship.

## GROW IT OR MOW IT

Confidence requires fear. Knowing what the object of our fear is, when it isn't God, allows us to understand what is happening in our hearts and develop a plan for change. The more we understand the object of our fear, the more our fear grows or wilts.

One of the steps I took to help beat the debilitating fear of flying was to learn how commercial airplanes are designed and tested. A key moment that changed my thinking about flying occurred when I discovered that hurricane hunters, the airplanes that fly right through to the eye of a hurricane, are normal cargo planes. They are modified with an array of scientific instruments, but the structure of the plane itself isn't changed at all. If you've ever seen a video of one of these planes in action, it looks like they are flying in a blender. The plane is bouncing violently up and down, and side to side. One plane endured sustained forces of 5.6 G's. As a point of comparison, most humans lose consciousness at 5.0 G's. Sustained forces of .0.1 or 0.2 G's would cause passengers and drinks to start floating around the cabin. In fact, the greatest danger to the crew during their flight through that particular hurricane was from the equipment that started flying around inside the plane.

The next time you get on a plane, know that it's designed to withstand much greater forces than you're ever likely to experience. No commercial pilot will see a normal thunderstorm, much less a hurricane, on the horizon and say, "Okay, here we go. Let's go chase that one. Everybody sit down and buckle up."

Understanding something about airplane design helped mow down my fear of flying, because now it was informed by facts. When it looks like the wings are flapping in the midst of turbulence, ordinarily I would freak out thinking they were about ready to bust right off. Then I discovered they're actually designed to work that way. The more information you know about whatever it is you revere or fear, the more that fear will either grow or wilt. If you're afraid of something that doesn't deserve your fear, learn more about it and your fear will diminish. If you revere something that deserves your fear, which is really only God, the more you know about him, the more your faith in him (the fear of the LORD) will grow, crowding out all other fears.

## CHAPTER 4
# CONFIDENCE REQUIRES STRESS

If you're like me, you think you need more stress like you need another hole in your head. We live in a world of constant stress. It starts when our alarm jangles us awake in the morning, continues through our commute, increases throughout our day at work or school, and only finally ends when we sink into a blissful unconsciousness that night. Unless we have nightmares. You might be surprised to know that confidence requires stress. As we'll see, that's ultimately good news.

### ONE THING

The Bible only identifies one thing, without which it is impossible to please God. Stress. No, that's not right. It's faith. Yes, faith.

Here is how the author of the book of Hebrews says it.

> *And without faith it is impossible to please him, for whoever would draw near to God must believe that he*

*exists and that he rewards those who seek him. (Hebrews 11:6)*

Our faith is so important to God that he grows it and purifies it, and that almost always includes stress of one kind or another. Almost nothing in the physical world grows strong and robust without stress. Imagine you've decided to start a workout regimen. Knowing the only way to get stronger is by stressing the muscle, you decide to start with bicep curls. Your first workout, you use two 5-pound barbells, one in each hand. You do five curls with each arm, then you rest. Then you do it again. Then you rest. Then you do it once more. Now you've completed three sets of five reps with each arm. You do this three times a week.

After six weeks, you feel like it's getting pretty easy. Your biceps have adapted to the stress of lifting five pounds, 15 times. You're now stronger, but your muscles won't continue growing unless you increase the stress. You start using 10 pound barbells, five reps, and three sets. Another four weeks go by and you feel like you could lift 10 pounds with each arm all day long. So you increase it to 15 pounds.

Now let's imagine another scenario. You've just been hit by a car. (Sorry, I wasn't watching where I was going.) You lie unconscious in a hospital bed for two weeks. When you wake up, you find it very difficult to move. Why? Because your muscles haven't had to work in 14 days. They've atrophied and need to relearn how to move.

Faith works in this exact same way. It's like a muscle.

You stress it appropriately and it grows. Leave it unstressed and it atrophies. God cares deeply about the health of our faith. So much so, that he is willing to put us under a great deal of stress to ensure that our faith grows strong and robust.

I have a picture on my computer of Navy SEALs in training. I'm referring to the men and women in the Navy special forces, not the sleek animals with the cute little noses. In the picture, a group of candidates, clothed in shorts and t-shirts, are springing off the bottom of a deep pool to catch a breath of air before they sink back down to the bottom again. How do I know they'll sink back down to the bottom? Because their hands are tied behind their backs and they have large weights tied around their ankles.

I can imagine the conversation with the training instructor before this little bit of terror. "Okay, here's what will happen next. We're going to weigh you down, cuff your hands behind your back, and throw you into a 10-foot pool. We want to see you jump off the bottom, take a breath, sink back down, jump off the bottom, take a breath, sink back down, for as long as you possibly can."

"What? Why?" you ask.

"We want to put you under as much physical and emotional stress as we can."

"Um, and why would I want to do this?"

"If your boat gets hit," the trainer says, "and you're in the water and under enemy fire, this may be the only way you survive. When that day comes, you can't freak out. I want you to have experienced this kind of stress before you're dodging enemy bullets behind enemy lines."

"Oh. Okay, let's do it."

What part of the military has the most difficult training? The special forces. In fact, the Navy SEALs training is so intense they have a 75% drop out rate. The special forces get the toughest training. They also get the toughest assignments.

There are different types of stress and different causes of stress. If you're the kind of person who just can't say no, which causes you to be always stressed about being over-committed, the solution is to learn to say no. If your boss is a slave driving narcissist who only sees you as a means of attaining his next promotion, you may need to think about looking for a new gig. In both of these circumstances, God wants to build your faith. He wants you to have enough faith in him to be able to say no without being afraid you're going to hurt the other person's feelings or worrying what they will think of you. He wants you to have the kind of faith in him that allows you to see possibilities for your life other than suffering under an abusive boss until he gets promoted out of your chain of command or dies of a heart attack.

The type of stress you're experiencing may be totally out of your control. There's little you can do to change a cancer diagnosis, a child turning away from the Lord, a pink slip in your mailbox, or a death in the family. But it can help to know that if God has allowed this kind of hardcore stress in your life, you've likely just started special forces training.

Sometimes God allows stress in our lives to convince us to quit putting confidence in ourselves. We need to get to the end of ourselves so that we will look at God. As long as I can meet my own needs, I don't need faith. But when God allows me to experience circumstances in which I can't meet my own needs, well, that's where faith begins.

> *For we do not want you to be unaware, brothers, of the affliction we experienced in Asia. For we were so utterly burdened beyond our strength that we despaired of life itself. Indeed, we felt that we had received the sentence of death. But that was to make us rely not on ourselves but on God who raises the dead.*
> *(2 Corinthians 1:8-9)*

There are two things to notice in these verses. First of all, does God ever give us more than we can handle? Absolutely. All the time. Paul says they were so afflicted that they were burdened beyond their strength. So much so, that they thought they were going to die. And that's the apostle Paul talking. Already in his ministry, he had been kicked out of town, imprisoned, whipped, beaten, stoned and left for dead. He was no wilting flower. He knew how to endure, but even he said things were so bad he thought he was going to die. Notice the reason for his hardship. He says the reason God did this was to make them rely not on themselves, but on God who raises the dead. God was training them. He was allowing this stress in their life, so they would stop relying on themselves and start relying on God. What does it take to rely on God?

Faith.

God is building their faith, building their confidence.

He's not hoping they will have more self-confidence. In fact, that's the opposite of what he's doing here. He's helping them turn from self-confidence to God-confidence. Why? Because only God can raise the dead. Only God has the power to get us through this broken, pain-filled world.

If you look closely, you can almost see Paul smirking as he writes this. It's like he's saying, "Yeah, we thought we were going to die. God did this to increase our faith in God who raises the dead." He's being sardonic, saying, "Even if we had died, God could have raised us from the dead." Not that Paul really expected that's what would have happened, but God is so powerful he can raise the dead. He's done it before. He is the only one who deserves to be the object of our faith. Paul, with tongue in cheek, makes that connection for us to help us get our eyes off ourselves and put our confidence in God.

## PERFECT CONFIDENCE

Earlier we said that the formula for confidence is performance over time. If that's true, then perfect confidence requires perfect performance over time. Where can we find perfect performance? God. If God's performance is perfect every time, then we can be perfectly confident in God every single time. Never a doubt. That doesn't mean we always achieve that level of confidence, but it's possible.

We spent the first chapter of this book breaking down self-confidence, explaining why it's a dead end because our performance is erratic at best. God-confidence is confidence in someone outside of ourselves. When our confidence is in someone who is perfect, whose track record is unblemished, whose power is unequaled, whose knowledge is complete, we can be one hundred percent confident, one hundred percent of the time. That's why God-confidence beats self-confidence every time.

The day will come when I'll be able to look back on this incredibly difficult circumstance I'm walking through with joy. Why?

> *And we know that for those who love God all things work together for good, for those who are called according to his purpose. (Romans 8:28)*

We may not feel it in the moment, we may not be able to see it at the time, but what God has allowed into your life, he will use for your good.

> *Count it all joy, my brothers, when you meet trials of various kinds, for you know that the testing of your faith produces steadfastness. And let steadfastness have its full effect, that you may be perfect and complete, lacking in nothing. (James 1:2-4)*

James uses the word "count." Count it all joy. In other words, put it in the joy column. It's an accounting term. Put this one in the joy column. I might not feel joy about it right now, but someday we'll look back on this with joy seeing how God worked it all together for his glory and our good.

GOD-CONFIDENCE

## OUR SHEPHERD

*A Psalm of David. The LORD is my shepherd; I shall not want. He makes me lie down in green pastures. He leads me beside still waters. He restores my soul. He leads me in paths of righteousness for his name's sake. Even though I walk through the valley of the shadow of death, I will fear no evil, for you are with me; your rod and your staff, they comfort me. You prepare a table before me in the presence of my enemies; you anoint my head with oil; my cup overflows. Surely goodness and mercy shall follow me all the days of my life, and I shall dwell in the house of the LORD forever.*
*(Psalm 23:1-6)*

Where is the psalmist when he writes these words? He mentions three locations. He's in the valley of the shadow of death; he's in the presence of his enemies; and he's dwelling in the house of the LORD. How can these all be true?

The Psalmist recognizes that he's going through a difficult and dangerous time. He's truthful about the harsh reality he faces. He's not Pollyanna-ish about it. He's real. He says, "I'm in the valley of the shadow death. I am in the presence of my enemies. But I'm also in the house of the LORD because God is with me. Even in the valley of the shadow of death, I fear no evil; even in the presence of my enemies, you prepare a table before me because you're with me. I'm in the presence of the LORD."

This is God-confidence: When we accurately

acknowledge all the chaos and danger around us—we don't pretend it's any less than it is—but we see how much greater God, and his purposes are in comparison.

## SECTION TWO
# GOD'S GOODNESS

There's an old gospel call and response that goes like this.

Pastor: "God is good."

Congregation: "All the time."

Pastor: "All the time?"

Congregation: "God is good!"

Although it may be true that God is good all the time, our ability to trust his goodness can fluctuate. Our past hurts or present circumstances can make it feel like he's anything but good. In this section we'll look at four ways God has demonstrated his goodness toward us and how those demonstrations can increase our confidence in his desire to be good to us all the time.

## CHAPTER 5

# GOD SACRIFICED FOR US

I grew up in a house where God was worshiped and taught, but somehow I grew up with a warped view of what God is like. A great pastor and author from the first half of the 20th century named A. W. Tozer once said, "What comes into our minds when we think about God is the most important thing about us."[3] What comes into your mind when you think about God? What do you think God is really like?

This is why doctrine and theology are vitally important. God cares a great deal about what you believe about him. Because what you believe about him will determine how you think, feel, and act on every other issue.

### LOVING, BUT NOT GOOD

When I was growing up, my dad had problems with anger and control. He was a serious Type A personality who was very old-school in his thinking about kids. He believed kids should be seen and not heard. They should respect their parents just because they were parents, regardless of how the parents treated their kids. Unfortunately, he didn't want to do anything that I enjoyed. I liked being outdoors and playing almost any sport you could name. The only time he went outdoors was to mow the lawn or weed the garden. We never went fishing, never watched basketball together on the television. He would demand that I help him with his home improvement projects, but I was all thumbs and couldn't remember which way to tighten or loosen a screw. When I was diagnosed as an adult with ADHD, much of my childhood years finally made sense. I was a hyperactive kid who always wanted to have fun. He was a serious-minded adult who believed fun was probably of the devil.

They say that your view of your earthly father seriously colors your understanding of what God is like. That was definitely true for me. I ended up with this really warped view of God. I didn't have any problem believing that God is all-powerful. He's omnipotent; he's great; and he's mighty. But, I really struggled to believe that he is good. I believed he "loved" me, but what that really meant was that he was going to do a lot of things to me "for my own good" that I was going to hate. I assumed most of those things would be painful. That was my experience with my dad. "This is gonna hurt me more than it hurts you" and "Someday you'll thank me" were his ways of saying, "I love you."

Now let me hasten to say that my dad is a very different person now. Shortly after I got married, he started going to a 12-step group. When he was working on step 8 (apologize and right wrongs) we had a long, intense conversation in which he owned many of the things that happened as I was growing up. That's part of why I share the stories of my childhood, because those stories are really about what God has done to transform both my life and my dad's, bringing reconciliation to the two of us, and helping us see God more like he really is.

## CURLY'S ADVICE

In the 1991 movie City Slickers, Billy Crystal plays Mitch, an overstressed yuppie looking for the meaning of life on a tourist's cattle drive. Jack Palance plays Curly, an old cowboy who's tougher than the leather your Bible is bound with. At one point in the movie Curly looks at Mitch and says,

"Do you know what the secret to life is?" Holding up one finger he says, "This."

"Your finger?" Mitch replies.

"One thing. Just one thing. You stick to that and the rest follows."

"But, what is the 'one thing'?" Mitch asks frustratedly.

With a knowing smile, Curly says, "That's what you have to find out."

What? That's it? Yeah, so Curly's really no help at all. Except he is right that there really IS one thing that's the secret to life. Since he wouldn't tell you what it is, I will.

The secret to life is figuring out how to connect the dots between who God is (his character, attributes, promises, and actions) and who we are (our identity, situation, and privileges in Christ). We live best at the intersection of God's Word and our world. It isn't easy, but it's true. The more time we can spend understanding God, studying theology, the better off we'll be.

Now before you slam this book shut and throw it in the burn pile, let me explain. A few of us are called to read big fat books written by scholars and write papers that use $10 terms like "hypostatic union" and such. Academicians play an important role in the church. I'm glad God calls some people to that life, but most Christians aren't. Still, we all need to know what God is truly like. That's all theology really is, right, the study of God? Whenever you ask yourself any variation of, "I wonder what God is like?" You're doing theology. You are a theologian. You might not be a scholar, but you're a theologian. You're doing theology.

In the last section, I shared how learning more about how airplanes are designed and built informed my fear of flying. The same is true of God. The more we learn about him, about who God is, what he's said, and what he's done, the more confident we will be in him. In this section and the next we're going to look at the two main facets of God, his goodness and his greatness. Then we'll connect the dots to our everyday life. Let's start with his goodness.

## THE MOST COMMON WORRIES

What do you think the most common worries are? I use the word worries rather than fears, because when we start listing fears, we bring up everything from public speaking to tarantulas. While those are real fears people have, most of us don't spend all our time worrying about them. Many of us spend a lot of time worrying about a few core things. What are they? Health, the future, finances, kids, or what other people think? Am I good enough? How will I die? The list can go on and on, but I think we can boil all of them down into four main concerns. Four basic questions can sum them up.

The first one is, Am I worth loving? Our identity is the key issue underlying this question. All the questions we ask about how other people think of us fit here. Does she really like me? Did they like my presentation? Will I know anyone at the party? How do my biceps look in this shirt? Does this dress make me look fat? Should I try to grow a beard?

The second question is, Do I have what it takes? Underlying this question is the concept of performance. It's revealed in questions like, Will I get the job? Am I a good parent? Can I pass this class? Do I really add anything to this team?

The third question is, Will I be okay? or Will he or she be okay? The key issue underlying this question is whether pain is right around the corner. Under this category are concerns like, Will my kids get good grades? Will my mom's surgery be successful? Will my son go to church at college? Will my girlfriend be safe on her trip to Africa? What will we do after the divorce? Will I ever get this debt paid down? How many layoffs will there be?

The fourth question is, Is all this worth it? Here the underlying issue is investment. We want to know that all the time, blood, sweat, and tears that we invest in this life will obtain the desired outcome.

Will I be okay? Am I worth loving? Do I have what it takes? Is all this worth it? If you could secretly ride around in your best friend's head for a day, you would hear some variation on one or more of these questions being asked again and again. You'll hear these questions even in the head of the most self-confident person you know. Our next step, then, is clear. We need to figure out how to live confidently while these four questions dog us every day.

We have already seen that consistently living with confidence requires our confidence be in someone who is absolutely consistent: God. As we dig deeper, we realize that our confidence in God needs to be based on two core beliefs. God is great and God is good. If he is great, but not good, then I believe he is powerful, but doesn't really have my best interests at heart. If he is good, but not great, then he might have my best interests in mind, but isn't truly capable of doing anything about it.

Digging still deeper we find that it's not enough to believe that God is generically good. We must believe that he wants to use his goodness on our behalf. For years, my problem was that I believed God was good in a general sense, but I didn't believe God wanted to be good to me personally. It has been a lifelong journey for me to discover how personally committed to me he is.

## TRUE LOVE

The greatest demonstration of God's love is his sacrifice on our behalf in Christ Jesus. God's sacrifice answers the core question, "Am I worth loving?"

Love may be a many-splendored thing, as the song says, but as we use it in English, it's also a very odd thing. We talk about loving our spouses and our children. Then, in the next sentence, we talk about loving pepperoni pizza or the cute cat picture on Facebook. If we're not careful, love can get confusing really fast. To be sure, for many it has.

Though we often talk about love as a feeling that comes and goes, those feelings are probably better understood as affection. True love is an active choice. It may or may not have nice feelings associated with it. True love is measured in units of sacrifice. When my wife and I meet with a couple for premarital counseling we ask each person, "How willing are you to sacrifice for this love?" Frankly, I'm not willing to sacrifice more than about six seconds of my time for that cute cat picture on Facebook, so that's a whole different kind of love than the love I have for my wife and daughter. Units of sacrifice. Jesus says there's no greater love than this, than to lay down your life, the ultimate sacrifice. That's why there's no greater love. If you're willing to die, it's off the charts. That's the most love you can show.

Another aspect of love we get confused about is that love always depends on the giver. Love does not depend on the receiver. If it does, it's not love. Why do I love my wife, Kathy? Do I love her because she does great things for me? I really enjoy the way she gets up in the morning with me and cooks me breakfast. She consistently makes perfect over medium eggs, which is really hard to do. Kathy is the kind of person who can eat eggs every morning of her life. I really like her eggs, but every morning for life? Most mornings we have eggs, and she serves me two perfect, over medium eggs. But, what happens when the yolk breaks and now it's an egg over hard? Do I love her less? Of course I don't, but let's raise the stakes a little. What happens if we get in a car accident and she gets both arms amputated and can never make eggs again. She can never do my laundry. She can never give me a hug. Now how do I feel? What if that car accident is a little bit worse? Now she's in a coma for a year and wakes up with serious brain damage. She doesn't even remember who I am. What if she lives to be 90 and never remembers who I am? Do I love her less?

If my love for her relies at all on her, the answer is bound to be yes. I love her less. When couples separate you almost always hear some variation of, "You don't treat me like you did when we were first married. You don't do the things I want you to do. You don't show me love in a way that I want you to show me love." This is true for spouses. This is just as true for friends. It's also true for coworkers. It's true for any relationship where love is involved. If the relationship is based on how you treat me, on what I get from you, it's not love. Love is always about what I give to you. Love is my commitment to seek your best in every situation. That's what I commit myself to.

On January 20th, 1990, I made a commitment to love my wife for the rest of my life. Last month we celebrated our 30 year anniversary. Many of those years have been wonderful, but we've had some really tough times as well. We are both honest about that because we've seen people try to pretend everything in their relationship is fine and things just spiral out of control. We've had to seek help. We've had counseling, We've had wonderful friends involved in our lives and our relationship. We made it through 30 years, praise God. But, if I start getting selfish tomorrow? Any relationship can succeed and any relationship can fail.

Simply saying, "I love you" on the day I got married isn't enough to see our marriage through. I also have to wake up every single day and say it again, make that same commitment. On January 20th, 1990, I made a lifetime commitment, but that commitment doesn't mean anything unless I renew it every single day. I'm going to stay married regardless of what she does. My love for Kathy is fully dependent on me.

When we really start to think about it, this makes sense. If we flip it and take that thinking to its logical conclusion we get this: I love you. As long as you give me what I want. As long as you make my perfect eggs over easy, I'll love you. You stop that? I'll love you less. You stop taking out the garbage? You act differently now than you did when we were dating? Life circumstances get harder? I get a bit more insecure? Well, then everything is up for grabs.

If anything can change my love for Kathy, where does that put her? It puts her on thin ice. Right? That's not love. That's manipulation. That's me saying you'd better do what I want in order for me to keep loving you. Yet, that's what the world says love is. If you can fall in love, you can fall out of love. "My spouse isn't the same person," we say. "We just grew apart." Nonsense. It's harder than hard to love somebody, and it's super hard over a long period of time. But that's what love is. Love is hardcore, and it's measured in units of sacrifice. How much am I willing to sacrifice for this person every day, every day, every day, for the rest of my life? The easy example is with a spouse, but it's the same with a friend, right? If I'm only committed to my friends as long as there's something in it for me, then I don't really love them. I'm just being selfish. If I'm committed to them for the long haul, day by day by day, because I have made that choice, irrespective of what they do, then I'm starting to understand what love is.

If love depends on the giver, when God says, "I sacrificed for you," his love for you is not based on you—at all. It's based one hundred percent on God. "Love" that depends on the person receiving love, results in both sides manipulating each other. She will always try to manipulate me to get my love. I will always try to manipulate her by withholding or showing my love based on how she pleases me. It's this horrible, codependent, manipulative game, yet we all know people who live like that. If you're one of them, stop it. Love.

> *God shows his love for us in that while we were still sinners, Christ died for us. (Romans 5:8)*

How does God demonstrate to us that he is good and wants to be good to us, personally? "While we were still sinners, Christ died for us." God paid the ultimate price in Christ to show us his love. It was ultimate, not just because it was death, but it was death while we were sinners, while we were in open rebellion against God. Paul says in the verses just preceding this one, that for a good person, someone might be willing to sacrifice their own life, but for an enemy, for someone who's actively rebelling, for someone who's basically flipping you off? Forget it. I'm not going to die for you. I'm not gonna do anything for you. Go fix your own self. But God demonstrates his love for us in that while we were still sinners, Christ died for us. When we minimize how sinful we were before God saved us, we minimize the lavishness of his grace which he gave us.

## AM I WORTH LOVING?

The next question we ask is, am I worth loving? The answer is, your lovability is irrelevant. Why? Because you are loved. You are loved with the perfect, complete, whole, everlasting love of God, which will never go away. You can't out-sin God's love. You can't out-fear God's love. You can't out-rebel God's love. There's nothing you can do as a believer in Christ that will take you out of God's love.

> *Who shall separate us from the love of Christ? Shall tribulation, or distress, or persecution, or famine, or nakedness, or danger, or sword? (Romans 8:35)*

> *My Father, who has given them to me, is greater than all, and no one is able to snatch them out of the Father's hand. (John 10:29)*

Your lovability is not an issue. God didn't start loving you based on your worth, and he's not going to stop loving you based on your worth. Well, what if I quit obeying? Well, that's a problem. If you quit obeying God, that really is a problem, but it's not going to make him love you less. He may nudge you a bit to get you back on track. He may bring some people into your life to tell you the truth. He may allow you to reap the consequences of that rebellion to motivate you to turn around, but he's not gonna love you less.

Your lovability is beside the point. He didn't send Jesus because you were worth it. Frankly we weren't worth it. We were still dead in sin. Paul says in Ephesians 2:5 that while we were still dead in our sins, that's when he made us alive.

Christ died for us when we were worthless. That's when he paid the price for our sin. It wasn't because of anything in us, everything was in God.

We may think, "Well, that doesn't make me feel very good about myself." Okay, but that's not the point. The point is you don't have to worry about yourself.

Decades of focusing on self-esteem have taken us down a dead end path. We have been duped into thinking that the way to feel good about ourselves, the way to feel confident in ourselves, is to believe that we're okay just the way we are. But then, every single one of us has the same experience. We look into ourselves and find that we're not okay. We don't like ourselves, and for good reason. How can I be confident when there's all this mess inside? We basically have two options. We can fake it till we make it, which is basically what current psychological theory, as well as Oprah, the media, and just about everyone else you might find, would have us do. Or we can admit reality and look for some kind of help outside of ourselves.

It's at this point that most of us make one of two choices. We either choose the road of high performance, seeking to suppress the truth about what's inside by getting really good at something. Or we choose the road of relationships, looking for someone else to tell us that we're really okay inside, even when we know we aren't. Of course, some of us are overachievers. We try to choose both roads simultaneously. This never works out over time.

The great news of the gospel is that your lovability is irrelevant. You. Are. Loved

## MAKE IT REAL

One of the sins I really struggle with is overeating. It's tricky, because everyone overeats sometimes. It's not always a sin, but for me, I overeat to find joy and comfort, both of which I should be finding in God rather than food. When I have a bad eating day and I've just consumed six pepperoni pizzas and nine strawberry cheesecakes (okay, not literally ... not every time anyway), I feel like there's this great chasm between me and God. Now, is it a good idea for me to repent and say, "God, I'm sorry. I don't know what I was thinking. I come back to you"? Yeah, absolutely. But is God's love any less on a bad eating day than on a good eating day? No, of course not.

Maybe your issue is your temper. Things go wrong at work and KaBlooey! you just expelled a whole year's frustration on that poor little intern who is just trying to help. Now she's in tears and you're left trying to explain how a Christian can act that way.

Some people face less public struggles. It's been too long since you had any serious intimacy with your spouse and you're feeling shunned and alone. It's all too easy to look at websites you would never want your spouse—or anyone else for that matter—to see.

No matter what sin you struggle with, no matter how often you fail, God's love is pegged at one hundred percent maximum all the time. It will never change. Your lovability is irrelevant because you are loved. What would that do to your level of confidence if you really believed it? If we're right, and these four questions form the foundation of all our worries, then we've just wiped out twenty-five percent of the world's worries. The gospel is indeed good news.

Am I worth loving? It's not even the right question. The question we should ask is, "Am I loved?" God's answer is, "Yes, absolutely!" You are loved from the tippy top of your worried head to the very bottom of your frantic feet. You are perfectly loved by a perfect God who invites you every day to experience more and more of his love and goodness, which he's demonstrated in amazing ways.

"But," you may say, "I don't usually feel like it." Oh, of course not. Our feelings go up and down more than a thermometer in a Midwestern winter. However, the rock bottom reality is that God's love is solid, so we'll use that truth to inform our emotions.

## INFORM OUR EMOTIONS

Are you mad at God? Okay, that's fine. God can take it. It's just a feeling. Are you sad? Did God disappoint you? Okay, sometimes we're disappointed by those who love us. That's just an emotion. We don't belittle our emotions. They are important. They give us a peek at what's happening down deep in our souls. But we also don't put all our eggs in that basket. Emotions can be based on reality or they can be based on misinformation. We acknowledge our emotions, but then we ask where they are coming from. Are they based on truth? If not, then we inform them.

Let's imagine that my wife just yelled at me from the other room. "John, get in here!" Immediately I feel angry. What is she yelling at me for? What did I do? Whatever she's upset about couldn't have been my fault. I feel my anger. I don't deny that I'm angry. I don't think that somehow as a Christian I should never get angry. I just feel it. Then I walk in the other room to see what's happening with Kathy. Once I get to the kitchen I am met with a wall of smoke and the scent of burning oil. Somehow whatever Kathy was cooking started a fire in the kitchen. Why the smoke alarm didn't go off, I do not know, but somebody needs to call 911 immediately.

Am I still angry? Of course not. My emotions were fed new information that helped them understand that Kathy wasn't angry at me about something. She was scared and needed my help. Right away, thank you!

That's how emotions work. They respond to what we feed them. Too often we let our emotions run rampant without asking the question, "What is this feeling based on?" and then hunting down the data we need to inform our emotions and pull them into line with the truth.

Whether or not I feel loved by God doesn't change for a minute whether or not he loves me. Whether or not I feel like he's good at any particular time in my life doesn't change the fact that he is good. When we don't feel God's love and goodness, we can inform our emotions by reading Scriptures that reveal God's character. We can read psalms that celebrate his deliverance and commitment to his people. We can meditate on the gospel narratives about Jesus' death and resurrection. We can allow Paul's words from the first three chapters of Ephesians to soak into our hearts. We can listen to Jesus' words in the first three chapters of Revelation as he describes what he has in store for us in heaven.

God is good. All the time. Let's tell it to our hearts.

CHAPTER 6

# GOD GRACED US

As I write these words from my home just outside Chicago, the Chicago Bulls basketball team is looking pretty iffy. They've won 19 games and lost 36. They're in tenth place out of 15 teams in their conference. I'm a true fan, so I've decided I'm going out for the team. I'm 51 years old. I weigh a little bit more (okay, a lot more) than I should. I've had three back surgeries, one of which was a spinal fusion, and I may or may not have broken my foot recently.

How much help do you think I'm going to be to the Chicago Bulls? I was a pretty good basketball player when I was nine. They say there's this thing called muscle memory. Maybe it will all come back?

I go to the Bulls workout facility and there in the locker room sits Michael Jordan.[4] Michael confides in me that he has stage four basketball cancer and no medicine or treatment will help. Amazingly, the basketball gods have determined that he'll go to basketball heaven on one condition. If, as his final act on earth, he imparts all of his basketball powers to someone totally unworthy to receive them, then he'll go to basketball heaven. Right then and there he gives me all of his basketball powers. I now have all the powers of Michael Jordan. Now how much good will I be to the Chicago Bulls?

God graced us. I know grace isn't really a verb, but I think using it this way is helpful to understand the depth of what God has done. You may have heard the word GRACE used as an acronym. It stands for God's Riches At Christ's Expense. The core question that God's grace answers is, Do I have what it takes?

## AMAZING GRACE

> *Blessed be the God and Father of our Lord Jesus Christ, who has blessed us in Christ with every spiritual blessing in the heavenly places, (Ephesians 1:3)*

You have every spiritual blessing that exists in Christ Jesus. Why? Because you are in Christ Jesus and he is in you. You've been forever united to him. He's in you. You're in him. You have all of Christ's riches in your bank account. One of the metaphors for our union with Christ is that of a bride and a groom. In the same way that a bride and groom are called to share everything in common, so Jesus shares everything with us. We are his bride and his is our groom.

Paul goes on in the first part of Ephesians to say that we have the same power in us that God used when he raised Jesus Christ from the dead. That's a lot of power. That's the power that you have, and that's only one of your riches in

Christ. You have God's power at your disposal. God gave us his own riches at Christ's expense.

## THE GRACEMOBILE

Several years ago, my wife and I were living in South Dakota and she was working as a certified nurse's assistant in a nursing home. Her shift started at five o'clock in the morning, which meant she had to wake up earlier than that to get ready and drive to work. We've always been a one-car family, which means if I needed the car that day, I had to get up and drive her to work at zero dark thirty in the morning.

I'm not a morning person. My peak time is from about eleven in the evening to three in the morning. Working at a church, those hours don't go over so well. They want their pastor around when they're actually awake, so it's a bit of a compromise. I wake up in time to get to the office at a decent hour, and they don't complain that I'm not fully functional until around noon. I was exhausted at just the thought of having to drive Kathy to work that early in the morning a couple days a week, Then, a miracle happened. Just like those movies by Disney. Someone in the church gave us a car. Oh, we were so very, very grateful.

Gordy's car was an old Toyota Camry, a decent car. His family used it as what they called a "farm car." That's the car that you take out over the fields when it's too far to walk. Mostly the car was just sitting around waiting for their son to turn 16 because it was going to be his car, so Gordy gave us this car as an indefinite loan. We weren't really having any problems with it, but after a month or so the sticker on the windshield said it was time to get the oil changed.

I called Gordy and said, "Hey, we've got to get an oil change on your car. Where do you normally take it?"

To which he replied, "Oh, I'll take it. Don't worry about it." He came over, grabbed the car, got the oil changed, and brought it back. We didn't have to pay for the oil change.

Then something happened to it. I forget exactly what was wrong. It was a fairly small thing, but it still needed to get fixed.

"Oh, I'll fix that," Gordy said. He picked up the car, brought it to the mechanic, and got it fixed. We basically owned this car and didn't have to pay for anything except gas the entire time we used it. Gordy's car at Gordy's expense. You might say it was actually at Gordy son's expense because we were putting mileage on the car he was going to get. That's grace, right? It's a wonderful picture of grace. Gordy did not have to do that for us. We did not deserve it. He just did it because he's a great guy, and he cared about us.

## GRACE, BY DEFINITION

God's riches belonged to God. There was no reason for him to share them with anyone, least of all rebel sinners like us. Notice the flow of thought in Paul's letter to the Ephesians as he explains how God gave us his riches.

> *And you were dead in the trespasses and sins in which you once walked, following the course of this world, following the prince of the power of the air, the spirit that is now at work in the sons of disobedience—among whom we all once lived in the passions of our flesh, carrying out the desires of the body and the mind, and were by nature*

> *children of wrath, like the rest of mankind. But God, being rich in mercy, because of the great love with which he loved us, even when we were dead in our trespasses, made us alive together with Christ—by grace you have been saved—and raised us up with him and seated us with him in the heavenly places in Christ Jesus, so that in the coming ages he might show the immeasurable riches of his grace in kindness toward us in Christ Jesus. (Ephesians 2:1-7)*

First he describes us as being dead in our trespasses and sins. Obviously, we weren't physically dead, so he must mean that we were spiritually dead. We didn't have the ability to relate to, please, and communicate with God. In the same way a physical corpse really isn't able to do anything except rot, when we were spiritually dead, we weren't able to do anything spiritually worthwhile.

At the end of that first sentence he says that we were not only dead, but we were, "by nature children of wrath." That may seem harsh at first, but recognize why we deserved wrath. We bought into this broken world's way of doing things. We were following the devil (the prince of the power of the air). We were living life for our own pleasure, period. Though we may not have wanted to admit it, even the good things we did were based indirectly on selfish motives. Our sin hurts us and other people, so we deserved punishment.

Then come two of the most wonderful words in Scripture, "But, God." When we were helpless and hopeless, God made us alive together with Christ. Two thousand years ago when God raised Jesus from the dead physically, he reached forward through time and raised you from the dead spiritually. Not only that, but he raised us up with Christ and seated us with him on his heavenly throne. Why? Because we had what it takes? No! At that time we didn't have anything good in us. It was because of his rich mercy and great love for us. Not only that, but he wanted to be able to spend all eternity showing the immeasurable riches of his grace in kindness toward us.

When we deserved God's wrath, he chose instead to freely give us his riches. Though the gift was free to us, it cost Christ everything. The cross paid it all. God's Riches At Christ's Expense.

Grace, by definition, is free to the one who receives it. I cringe whenever I hear someone talk about "cheap grace." Grace is not cheap. Grace cost the Father the death of his own son. Jesus willingly suffered and died, taking the punishment for our sins. There was nothing cheap about it. It is free to us, but very expensive for God, in Christ.

## YOUR ABILITY

So back to our core question, "Do I have what it takes?" Am I up to the challenge now that I'm saved? How should I feel about myself? Here's the answer. Your ability is irrelevant. Why is your ability irrelevant? Because inside of you lives someone whose ability is omnipotent. The Holy Spirit is inside of you, and his ability is without equal. It's perfect. You can accomplish anything he wants you to accomplish. He's God, and his ability has been given to you. (See especially Ephesians 1:18-21)

Now, let me be quick to say, I don't mean that we

ignore aptitude when we choose what kind of commitments to make. If you can't carry a tune, please don't go talk to your worship leader and say you want to be on the worship team. If you struggle with math, it's probably best not to make it a goal to teach advanced physics. God has created us with certain aptitudes, and we need to wisely live within the realm of what's possible for each of us. The scenario I'm talking about is this: When you have been faithful and you're facing something fearful, do you have what it takes to overcome? Well, it's irrelevant. You may succeed or you may fail. Whichever thing happens, God will ensure that you'll be able to look back on it and be glad it turned out the way it did.

See, it's not that God's always going to swoop in like Superman and make everything great, and you're never going to fail. Believe me, I fail a lot. I also tell my staff to fail. I tell my friends to fail. When I do leadership coaching, I tell my clients to fail. Why? Because we're humans. We're not omniscient. Failure means we didn't have enough information or skill. We did our best, but we still came up short. If we look back, we'll find somewhere there was a miscalculation in what we thought or did that we can likely learn from. There's nothing wrong with failure. It's not a sin. We may do our best, try our hardest, and God may allow us to fail. Then we'll be sad, but, I can deal with sadness and so can you. It's just a human emotion. You don't need to be destroyed over it. You need to inform your sadness that someday you'll look back on that failure and be thankful that it happened exactly as it happened because God is working all things together for your good. (Romans 8:28)

This assumes you were faithful and weren't doing something stupid. If I think I'm going to jump off the top of a skyscraper and fly over to my friend's house, then I'm just being an idiot. God's blessings don't include an insurance policy protecting you from your own idiotic choices. Assuming that we're listening to wisdom, doing our part to be faithful, and seeking God, our ability is irrelevant. Our earthly success or failure is irrelevant. What if you believed that? How confident would you be if you knew that your ability was beside the point because the results were in God's hands?

Whether or not you have what it takes is irrelevant. God has what it takes, and if he's led you to this, he's gonna make sure the outcome is what he planned. Even if it's uncomfortable for a season, you'll be able to look back on it and see that it was good and rejoice in it. What might you try if you knew this was true? How might you be willing to look foolish in the short term?

## MINIMUM VIABILITY

In my leadership coaching, I encourage people to consider the concept of minimum viability. You may be familiar with the idea of a minimum viable product. We experience it every day with our cell phones and our computers. Apple or Microsoft puts out a new software update, and it's the minimum viable product. It's the minimum product that will work to some degree. They know it's not perfect. They know it's not gonna work all the time. They know there are bugs. They've done what they can to get most of the bugs out, so they give it to us to start using. Then everybody starts complaining about it, right? "It won't do this. That is broken. It crashed my computer." Then they start to fix those issues, and over time it gets better and better. Why do they do that? Why do they roll out the product before it's perfect? Two reasons.

First, there comes a point in any creative process when you are no longer capable of seeing what's there. In the same way that every author needs an editor, every coder needs fresh eyes on their work. You just can't find everything that's wrong. A software developer has a sense of how the end user will utilize the product, so they test the software to make sure it is capable of doing them. Then, after the product is rolled out, they discover that users actually want to use the product in entirely different ways than the developer envisioned, and things start to go wrong.

Second, as you're testing and fixing and editing, you reach the threshold of diminishing returns. The cost of hunting down every small error and fixing them isn't worth what you can actually charge for the product. It becomes more economically viable to find what's wrong by getting it out in the hands of users. They start using it. They'll tell you what's wrong, and then you fix it.

Now we can have disagreements about where exactly that point should be. I often wish software developers would do a much better job before they ship. But in general, I think minimum viability is a philosophy that should be considered. If you live your life with a high value on excellence and believe that everything you do needs to be ready for prime time television, you're going to bear a heavy burden and quickly be on the road to burnout.

If you have reasonable expectations about the variety of activities you're engaged in, you'll be much more relaxed and happy. What's the minimum viability for prime time? Pretty darn good. Certain school or work projects probably need to meet this high level of excellence. On the other hand, what is the minimum viability for family dinner on a night everyone is exhausted? Maybe frozen pizza and premade salad is good enough.

How does this relate to God-confidence? The question is, "Do I have what it takes?" Do I have what it takes to write a book about God-confidence that will transform people's lives? Absolutely not. If this book transforms people's lives it will because God has moved, not because I had some great spiritual skill with words. I can't change your life, but in the end, my ability is irrelevant. Whether or not this book helps people depends mostly on God. That leaves me free to simply be faithful and leave the rest to him.

Whether you're an accountant, or a musician, or a business person, or a salesperson, or a a stay-at-home parent, you can have that same attitude in what you do. Choose the areas of your work and life that will get your best efforts. Focus on them, practice, add to your skills. Shoot for excellence. Then remember that at the end of the day, your work is a simple sacrifice to the Lord. Allow him to take it. Pray, "God, I did everything I knew how. I'm sure I made mistakes. I'm going to come back next week and discover how it all came out. I worked really hard and I leave it with you, and I'm gonna enjoy my weekend."

## CHAPTER 7
# GOD PROVIDES FOR US

In 2007 my family faced a perfect storm of financial crises. I started my own leadership consulting company early in the year. At first, I was able to get some pretty good clients, but as the year went on fewer and fewer companies were willing to spend money on consulting. We wouldn't know until the following year that we were facing the beginning of the worst financial crisis in global history.[5] I started looking for other work.

At the same time my wife lost her job. Then she started to have some serious health issues. She suffered through six surgeries in 12 months. This kept her from looking for a new job and threw us into a spiral of ever-increasing medical debt. By the end of the year we had to leave our apartment because we could no longer pay the rent. We were effectively homeless.

One evening just before Thanksgiving when life looked its bleakest, Kathy had a visit from a home-health nurse. Because of her surgeries, she required a nurse to come each evening to administer IV medication. The nurse who came this particular night hadn't been on the regular rotation. At the last minute she'd received a call asking if she could fill in for the woman who typically came.

We sat in the living room, my wife, our daughter, the nurse, and me. After she inserted the IV and got the medicine flowing, the nurse looked at the three of us and said, "You guys have had a tough go of it, huh?"

Not knowing what might be in Kathy's chart, we assumed she was talking about Kathy's surgeries. "Yeah," Kathy said, and proceeded to tell the nurse about the last several months' worth of surgeries.

"Yes, but it's bigger than that, isn't it?" The nurse asked. Then, without waiting for an answer she said, "Don't worry. I know God is going to provide for you."

Um ... what? That started a two-hour long conversation with this nurse who didn't know us at all. She told us very confidently that God loved us, had a plan for us, and that all this was going to eventuate in his glory and our good. And I thought I was supposed to be the preacher in the group!

That night literally changed our lives. Things didn't get better for us right away. In fact, they got quite a bit worse. A month later, we were evicted. Our pastor and his wife graciously let us (along with our two cats!) live with them, but it was very hard to explain to friends and family what was going on. "Why are you sleeping in your pastor's basement? How long has this been going on? What are you going to do next?" Answering the onslaught of questions over and over again made me want to stay in bed and never see anyone again. Except, I knew I had to go talk to people in order to find work. Finally, after several months I was invited to join the pastoral staff of a church in another state. That conversation with a nurse we never saw again was what got us through the darkest times. In fact, later, we gathered 12 small stones and put them in a glass jar as a way of remembering how God had provided for us at each step in our journey. (See 1 Samuel 7:12)

## IT'S IN HIS NAME

The third way God demonstrates his goodness to us is that he provides for us. His provision answers the key question, "Will I be okay?" Or, "Will she or he be okay?" This is the question on every parent's mind when they drop their child off at preschool for the first time. It's the question rising up from the pit of your stomach as you watch your parent being wheeled in for surgery. It's the question you ask when waving goodbye to your best friend as she boards the plane to take her to Nigeria for the summer. It's an important question, and not knowing the answer can often shake our confidence.

You may have heard that one of God's names is Jehovah-Jireh. It's Hebrew, of course, and means The LORD Will Provide. Provision is one of the names of God. It flows directly from his character, and yet, we often miss the ways God provides for us. Too often we relegate God's activity to the miraculous. Forgetting that every breath we take, every move we make, every new day, is a gift from his hands. God is certainly involved in miracles. He's equally involved in ensuring that the air around you right now is the correct mix of oxygen, nitrogen, argon, carbon dioxide, and methane.

Get those percentages off by even just a little bit and it will suddenly become very difficult to breath.

> *For by [Jesus] all things were created, in heaven and on earth, visible and invisible, whether thrones or dominions or rulers or authorities—all things were created through him and for him. And he is before all things, and in him all things hold together.*
> *(Colossians 1:16-17)*

By him all things hold together. All things. Jesus knows all the mysteries of science. He understands all the laws of quantum physics. He invented them. He is using them to ensure that the universe operates exactly as he wants it to. God is providing for you. Every time your heart beats, every time you sit down to eat a greasy burger and fries, every time you fall asleep at night, every time you're encouraged by your best friend's voice, God is providing for you. He provides rest, comfort, food (and the money to pay for it), health, and a million other gifts that we overlook every day. Let's not relegate God to the supernatural as if that's the only sphere that he can work in. Who makes it rain? Who makes it stop? Who gave you parents to raise you? Who gave you teachers to instruct you? It's all God. God provides for us.

    I remember as a kid saying these words to my mom, "You never do anything for me." If you are a mom, or had a mom, or know a mom, you can understand just how wrong that statement is. Meanwhile my mom was probably thinking "Hmm, I cook his food, buy his clothes, provide a roof over his head, pay for his toys, take him on vacations. I give him rides to band rehearsal, to his friend's house, to movies. I clean up after him and do his laundry ..." The list goes on and on of the things that a mother does for her child. What I should have said was, "Right this minute you aren't doing what I want you to do." How often do we think the same way of God? We fail to see the many, many things he does for us. We complain that he doesn't take care of us, and he still patiently, lovingly provides for us.

I'm following a new read-through-the-Bible-in-a-year plan. This year, as I got to Exodus, I was fascinated by the cycle of provision and complaint. God provides for the people of Israel, by bringing them out of Egypt. Then they complain and wail when they reach the Red Sea. God provides a way through the sea. Then they complain there's only bitter water to drink. God provides a way to purify the water. Next they complain there's nothing to eat. God provides manna from heaven. I mean, what's with these Israelites? Don't they understand that God has a great plan for them and will never, ever let them down?

What's with me? I mean, I'm one hundred percent exactly the same as the Israelites. "God," I complain, "I dunno how we're going to pay the bill. God, so-and-so is mad at me. God, this other person disappointed me. God, I'm not satisfied with my job." We get so upset because God doesn't give us what we want right now, rather than understanding all that God has already given us just by giving us life. Anybody who's ever seen the majesty of the Grand Canyon, swam in the vast ocean, stood next to a mighty mountain, driven through a barren desert, walked in a forest teeming with life, watched snow gently drift to the ground, held a newborn baby, looked into the eyes of a lover, lost themselves in laughter with a good friend, or felt the comforting arms of a parent, knows somewhere deep in their heart that God provides.

> *He who did not spare his own Son but gave him up for us all, how will he not also with him graciously give us all things? (Romans 8:32)*

If God was willing to give us his son, the most profound display of love ever seen, will he not also, with Jesus, give us everything? Of course he will. God demonstrated his provision when he planted Adam in a garden, put Noah in an ark, and caused a ram to wander over to see what Abraham was about to do to Isaac. He gave Moses (and us) a Sabbath rest, Elijah an adopted family, and Jesus a young child's lunch.

Adam's garden followed the natural laws of creation. The blueprints for Noah's ark were given through supernatural communication. It was total "coincidence" that the ram got stuck in a thicket right where Abraham was about to sacrifice Isaac. God uses all kinds of means to provide for us, but his provision is consistent.

## ASKING THE RIGHT QUESTION

Let's return to our key question, "Will I be okay?" There are two possible answers to this question, depending on what you mean when you ask it. If, when you ask, "Will I be okay?" you mean, "Will I be exempted from the normal dangers, risks, and harms of this world?" then the answer is a firm no. God has never promised to shield us from every evil in this broken world. But if you mean, "Will God work out what is best for me and those around me, ensuring that we will one day look back on these events with joy at how he worked all things together for our good?" Then the answer is yes, absolutely. The truth is that our temporary comfort is irrelevant. I know this sounds harsh at first, but it's actually very helpful. Our temporary comfort is irrelevant, but our Shalom is guaranteed.

Shalom is the Hebrew word for "peace." But it means more than just the absence of conflict. Its meaning includes the concepts of wholeness and flourishing. That is what God guarantees.

A key milestone in the spiritual maturity process, and an essential for living confidently in a chaotic world, is recognizing that I don't need to be comfortable all the time. Sometimes God chooses to allow pain into our lives. The sooner we accept that, the better off we'll be. Few of us have experienced the kind of physical pain the apostle Paul experienced. He suffered shipwrecks, hunger, unending hard work, beatings, imprisonment, stoning, and more. Apparently God was okay with that. How can that be? Because there was something more important to God than Paul's earthly comfort. What was it? It was Paul's faith. Faith, you'll remember, requires stress.

Faith grows fastest when we face more than we can handle. Paul and Silas were in a Philippian prison, having just been beaten to within an inch of their lives, when they started singing hymns of praise to God (Acts 16:25).

I don't think they were singing because they were such holy people that they were beyond feeling acute physical pain. I think it's because singing was the only thing they could do. They were in so much pain. They were so mad that they had been falsely accused, unlawfully whipped, and imprisoned. They were so sad thinking about what their tiny little flock was going to do without them. They were so ripped up physically. The only way to stay sane, the only way to keep from despair was to cry out to God in desperation and sing songs to him. What happened after that? Revival.

Our temporary comfort is irrelevant. Unshakeable confidence requires that we look beyond the comforts of this life to the certainties of the next. What will the test results say? How will Human Resources respond? What will my girlfriend say? Will I be okay? If your real question is, "Will the test results say I don't have cancer?" I can't answer that. If you're asking, "Will I get the job?" No one but God knows. If you want to know, "Will my girlfriend accept my marriage proposal?" There's no guarantee that she will. But, if your question is, "Will I be okay through whatever process God leads me as he brings me home to heaven?" that I can answer with 100% confidence.

If you're concerned about ultimate realities and your ability to thrive as a spiritual person, I can guarantee God will provide peace, joy, encouragement, and his own divine presence every step of the way. Will you and your loved ones be free from pain, sickness, and discomfort? No. In fact, I can pretty much promise you the opposite in this life. You'll have trials. You'll have troubles. You'll face problems, but God is up to something much, much better than ensuring our temporary comfort. And one day we'll look back and be glad that he was.

## WHY THIS, GOD?

Think about this for a moment. Jesus died on the cross for our sin some 2,000 years ago. Since then, more and more people have trusted in him for their salvation. Exactly none of them have been immediately raptured out of this world and taken into heaven to be with God. Instead, he has left all of us here to continue living out our natural lives. If your life has been anything like mine, it's been a bit of an up and down journey.

The question I have is this: Why does God leave us here? We know his ultimate purpose is to take us to live in eternal bliss with him in glory. So, why not cut to the chase? Why allow us to endure all this pain and hardship in the meantime? What is his purpose, anyway?

The answer I've always been given to this question is that he wants more people to be saved, and he wants us to tell them the gospel. I get that, but it doesn't really work for me. If that was his main purpose in leaving us here on earth, wouldn't more people be saved? If he keeps us here primarily as a way of bringing others to faith, the strategy seems a bit backwards.

Imagine if everyone went directly to heaven within 24 hours of trusting Christ. You repent and believe in Jesus and you know that in one day you'll be walking on streets that are golden. Wouldn't you take the 24 hours you have left to share the gospel with everyone you know? "Hey, Joe, I only have two hours left, and I really want you to join me with Jesus. Trust him and within one day all your problems will disappear. You'll see God face-to-face and enjoy his gifts and blessings for all eternity." That's an easy sell. Everyone I know would sign up for that. Especially if people were disappearing 24 hours after trusting Christ. You know, what's a hard sell? "Hi Joe. If you trust Jesus right now, the rest of your life will be filled with trials and tribulation. You'll be afflicted. People will make fun of your faith. Yeah, that's all. Want in?" Heck, no! I don't want that. Who would?

So if the primary reason God leaves us here isn't to spread the gospel, what is it? There is one aspect of our lives that God is more concerned about than anything else. The Bible is actually pretty clear about this, but somehow we often overlook it. Here's how the author of the book of Hebrews talks about it.

> *And without faith it is impossible to please him, for whoever would draw near to God must believe that he exists and that he rewards those who seek him.*
> *(Hebrews 11:6)*

There is only one thing that the Bible says you can't live without. One thing that, if you don't have it, it is impossible to please God. That's faith. To God, the most important thing about you is your faith. He wants you to have a strong, robust, unwavering faith. So much so, that he takes the time throughout our earthly lives to build it in us. Here's how the apostle Peter puts it.

> *Blessed be the God and Father of our Lord Jesus Christ! According to his great mercy, he has caused us to be born again to a living hope through the resurrection of Jesus Christ from the dead, to an inheritance that is imperishable, undefiled, and unfading, kept in heaven for you, who by God's power are being guarded through faith for a salvation ready to be revealed in the last time. In this you rejoice, though now for a little while, if necessary, you have been grieved by various trials, so that the tested genuineness of your faith—more precious than gold that perishes though it is tested by fire—may be found to result in praise and glory and honor at the revelation of Jesus Christ. (1 Peter 1:3-7)*

Whenever you ask the question, "Why this, God?" you can know that in every situation of your life, God's purpose is to build your faith. In many cases he's doing more than that, but we can be assured that one of his main purposes is that we have a strong, robust, unshakable faith in him. Why did God allow this pain into your life? To build your faith. Why does he allow evil people to succeed? To build our faith. Why do bad things happen to good people? To build our faith. Through every success, every failure, every high, every low, God is building our faith. In all the good times, all the hard times, through loneliness and friendship, health and sickness, God is building our faith. Understanding what God is doing makes it so much easier to endure this broken and pain-filled world. Nothing is happening by accident, everything is happening for the strengthening of our faith.

Without risk, there is no faith because if we know what's

going to happen, there's no need to trust, to have faith. Faith equals risk. The more risk, the more faith is required. It's risky to believe in a God who allows cancer. It's risky to believe in a God who allows suffering. It's risky to believe that God is accomplishing something good in your most agonizingly awful times, but God is doing something good. He's building your faith. Someday you will look back and thank God profusely for not doing it your way, for doing it his way, in spite of the agony that you may have to endure before then.

Our temporary comfort is irrelevant. Will I be okay? I dunno. I may leave my house this afternoon, trip off the curb, knock my head on the sidewalk, have a brain aneurysm, and arrive at the hospital DOA. I guess that wouldn't be a bad way to go. I mean, it's pretty quick, right? We're all going to go some time. Will I be okay? If by that I mean, "Will I be comfortable, healthy, enjoy conflict-free relationships, pay all my bills on time, see my kids graduate from great universities, get amazing jobs, and have healthy kids of their own?" Then the answer is, "Who knows?" But if I mean, "Can I have shalom? Can my faith grow? Can I be strong in the Lord? Can I be confident that what he's doing will result in tremendous good and overwhelming joy? Can I get through this season stronger than when I started?" Yeah, absolutely.

## CHAPTER 8
# GOD REWARDS US

I grew up in a home that believed virtue was its own reward. We were taught never to look for some external incentive to do the right thing. Other parents might pay their children to do chores around the house, but we were expected to chip in simply because we were part of the family. I guess there's some validity to that, but it certainly isn't how God works. No, God rewards us. Remember what the author of Hebrews says? You must believe that God exists and that he is a rewarder of those who seek him.

God rewards us. This addresses the core question, is it worth it? Is all this suffering and hardship worth it? In the end, will I be able to look back and say the pain I endured was small compared to the glory I now enjoy? Or will I be disappointed? Well, let's go to the end and see, shall we?

## JUDGMENT

*For we must all appear before the judgment seat of*

> *Christ, so that each one may receive what is due for what he has done in the body, whether good or evil.*
> *(2 Corinthians 5:10)*

At the end of the world, God will judge each person for what they've done. Those who have done evil will be judged for their evil deeds. Those who are righteous will be judged for their righteous deeds. However, because of the cross of Christ, there is no punishment left for the believer. Paul says it like this.

> *There is therefore now no condemnation for those who are in Christ Jesus. For the law of the Spirit of life has set you free in Christ Jesus from the law of sin and death.*
> *(Romans 8:1-2)*

If you're a believer in Christ, you can be confident that no matter how hard life gets, you are not being punished. All of the punishment that you deserved went to the cross. You will never be punished for anything. It all went to Jesus. So, if God will judge each person for what they've done, and there's no punishment left for us who trusts in Christ, what will God's judgment look like? For the believer, God's judgment has nothing to do with what we may have done wrong. It has everything to do with what is worth rewarding. You needn't fear the judgment. In fact, you can actually look forward to it, because it will determine the size of your reward. Again, Paul says it best.

*Now if anyone builds on the foundation with gold, silver, precious stones, wood, hay, straw—each one's work will become manifest, for the Day will disclose it, because it will be revealed by fire, and the fire will test what sort of work each one has done. If the work that anyone has built on the foundation survives, he will receive a reward. If anyone's work is burned up, he will suffer loss, though he himself will be saved, but only as through fire. (1 Corinthians 3:12-15)*

Here we see the first little piggy who has built a life made of wood and straw. Only in this version of the story, there is no wheezing wolf, it is the Lord, himself, who comes along with a match. As he lights it ablaze, the piggy escapes becoming grilled pork, but everything else is incinerated. For some believers, the judgment will be like that. They have trusted Christ. They're saved. Their eternal destiny is not in doubt, but because they built their lives with wood, hay, and stubble, they receive no reward.

Now it's the second little piggy's turn. (In this story there are only two little piggies. No wolf and two piggies.) This little piggy built her life out of gold and precious stones. Just like the first little piggy, she faces the judgment and it all burns. But in this case the burning doesn't destroy everything. It refines it. Her reward is the purest gold. The precious stones sparkle and dazzle in the light. Most importantly, she hears the Master say, "Well done, good and faithful servant." The degree to which you have built your life on Christ, you will receive a reward. God's going to judge everyone, but there is no punishment left for us. Our judgment determines the value of the reward we receive.

Scripture paints a picture of the judgment to motivate believers to live wisely, to store up for ourselves treasures in heaven. However, that isn't the picture most of us have in mind as we go about our lives. The picture we tend to actually live by looks more like this. Life is a giant basketball game. A small group of referees, probably angels dressed in black and white stripes, collect all the data on what we did with our lives—all the good things and all the bad things. At the end of the game of life, they add up all the points we scored (the good things we did) and then they subtract a point for each of the penalties we made (the bad things we did). If, after subtracting the penalties from the points, we end up with a positive number, then we get a reward. If we end up with a negative number, we go to purgatory to pay off our debt. That's how the vast majority of people in the world think about judgment. They live by this equation: "If points minus penalties is greater than zero, then God dispenses a reward." The more points we have left after the penalties have been subtracted, the bigger our reward.

But that's not how it works. Why? Well, first of all, there are no penalties for those who have trusted in Christ, because there's no more punishment left for us. We don't have to worry about penalties being subtracted. Second, all the wood, hay, and stubble in the world doesn't earn any points. No matter how good it may seem, how much we may enjoy it, how much other people say it's important, if it's not in line with God's priorities, it's just going to burn up. Only gold and precious stones earn points. When we seek the Lord our God, when we love him with all our heart, soul, mind, and strength, when we love our neighbors as ourselves, when we give to the poor and give justice to the oppressed, then we are storing up for ourselves treasures in heaven. When we don't do these things, we aren't storing up treasures in heaven. However, we also aren't earning demerits because all the demerits were wiped out when we received God's Riches At Christ's Expense.

Jesus told us to store up for ourselves treasures in heaven. The author of Hebrews said we must believe that God rewards those who seek him. The apostle Paul explains that the materials we build our lives with determine our reward. It's a clear theme throughout Scripture. Of course, no one knows exactly what the rewards and treasures will look like. Talk of gold and precious stones is surely a metaphor, but we know it will be incredible. In fact, it will be out of this world.

## PUNISHMENT

I often hear Christians talk about their difficulties as if God is punishing them. "I must have done something wrong, and this is God's way of punishing me." No. He's not. This is a lie from the devil. It may seem like it's not that big a deal, but it really cuts to the heart of the gospel. The apostle Paul says it like this:

> *There is therefore now no condemnation for those who are in Christ Jesus. For the law of the Spirit of life has set you free in Christ Jesus from the law of sin and death. For God has done what the law, weakened by the flesh, could not do. By sending his own Son in the likeness of*

> *sinful flesh and for sin, he condemned sin in the flesh, in order that the righteous requirement of the law might be fulfilled in us, who walk not according to the flesh but according to the Spirit. (Romans 8:1-4)*

There is no condemnation. There is no punishment left for you. Jesus took all the punishment that you deserved when he died for you on the cross. It's gone. We need to take the lie that God may be punishing us out of our heads and burn it out of existence. Either the cross was sufficient for our salvation, or we need to add to it by suffering ourselves. If we need to add to it, then what was the point of the cross in the first place? No matter what you are going through right now, if you are a believer in Jesus Christ, I can guarantee you that it has nothing to do with God punishing you.

So what is happening? There are four reasons that we might face suffering in this life. First, I may be suffering the natural consequences of something stupid I did. If I jump off a building, I'm gonna hurt myself. That's not God punishing me. That's me being stupid and reaping the natural results. If I make a bad business decision, I will suffer the consequences. That's not God punishing me, that's simply the natural result of a bad decision.

Second, God may be pruning me. In my book *Meaning: Cultivating a Life of Joy, Purpose, and Impact*, I explain the difference between punishment and pruning. Punishment is the result of an unbeliever's sin against God. Pruning is the result of a believer's obedience to God. According to Jesus' words in John 15, God prunes those who are already bearing spiritual fruit, not those who have sinned against him. We can think of pruning like the discipline it takes to be a world-class athlete or musician. It's not necessarily enjoyable at the time, but its purpose is to help us bear even more fruit. Pruning is never punishment, it's preparation for higher levels of spiritual effectiveness.

A third reason we may endure pain is the result of someone else's sin. If we are persecuted for our faith, hit by a drunk driver, or the victim of gender discrimination in the workplace, we are suffering because someone else is sinning. This doesn't seem fair, and, indeed, it isn't fair at the time. But, God has assured us that he will make up for this kind of pain.

> *For I consider that the sufferings of this present time are not worth comparing with the glory that is to be revealed to us. For the creation waits with eager longing for the revealing of the sons of God. For the creation was subjected to futility, not willingly, but because of him who subjected it, in hope that the creation itself will be set free from its bondage to corruption and obtain the freedom of the glory of the children of God. For we know that the whole creation has been groaning together in the pains of childbirth until now. And not only the creation, but we ourselves, who have the firstfruits of the Spirit, groan inwardly as we wait eagerly for adoption as sons, the redemption of our bodies. For in this hope we were saved. Now hope that is seen is not hope. For who hopes for what he sees? But if we hope for what we do not see, we wait for it with patience. (Romans 8:18-25)*

When compared to the glory we will experience for all eternity, the pain and suffering we endure here in this world is small and inconsequential. For now, we groan with all the rest of creation, waiting for everything to be put right. But, we can do so with patience, knowing that God will ensure that it will be well worth the wait.

The final reason we may suffer is simply because we live in a broken world. Disease, natural disasters, economic recessions, some experiences aren't the result of anyone's behavior, they are simply part of living in this fallen world. It's important to note that no matter what the cause of our pain, God will still redeem it. He will ensure that all things work out for the good of those who love him.

## REWARD

God is a rewarder of those who seek him. When we say, "Virtue is its own reward" we are contradicting Scripture in two ways. First, God promises rewards for those who seek him. Second, our virtuous behavior in Christ often leads to hardship in this world. When we expect to experience heaven on earth, we will always be disappointed.

> *If in Christ we have hope in this life only, we are of all people most to be pitied. (1 Corinthians 15:19)*

In this life we will have hardship. In this life we will have tribulation. In this life we will be afflicted. In this life we will suffer. In fact, as believers in Jesus, we make choices in this world that result in more hardship, more affliction, possible persecution, and difficulty. We give large amounts of our income to our church, to missions, and to the poor. We spend our free time engaged in serving others. We move our families to difficult, sometimes even dangerous places in order to share the gospel. Is this because we are a crazy group of masochists? No, actually, quite the opposite. We are willing to make sacrifices in this world to reap our reward in heaven. We are willing to literally give up our lives because we know what is coming in the next world. In this world a long life of comfort will last only 70, 80, maybe 90 years. We look forward to the world in which our comfort and enjoyment of Christ will last forever. We are focused on eternity. The more focused on eternity we are, the more sacrifices we're willing to make in this life.

Back to our key question, "Is it worth it?" Yes, it is worth it! No matter what you may suffer in this world, it is worth it when your hope rests securely in heaven. But, how do we make this shift to an eternal focus when this world is so tangible? It's not by somehow escaping this world that we experience life with Christ. We don't meditate our way to our happy place and pretend that everything is okay. It's not. No, we face the gritty realities of living in a broken and fallen world head on, but we do so with patience and confidence in the God who has promised an unbelievably spectacular eternity.

## GOD STORIES

To grow in God-confidence, listen to God stories. There are believers in every church who have amazing stories of God's faithfulness, provision, and love. Ask other Christians, "What's the most amazing thing God's ever done for you?"

and listen to what they say. Read through the Bible paying attention to the times when God provided for his people. Notice especially how many times God provided when people were complaining or rebelling.

> *One generation shall commend your works to another, and shall declare your mighty acts. On the glorious splendor of your majesty, and on your wondrous works, I will meditate. They shall speak of the might of your awesome deeds, and I will declare your greatness. They shall pour forth the fame of your abundant goodness and shall sing aloud of your righteousness. ... The LORD is righteous in all his ways and kind in all his works. The LORD is near to all who call on him, to all who call on him in truth. He fulfills the desire of those who fear him; he also hears their cry and saves them.*
> *(Psalm 145:4-7, 17-19)*

God-confidence grows as one generation tells the stories of God's work to another. Faith is built when we tell our God stories. "Faith comes from hearing and hearing by the word of Christ." (Romans 10:17) Our confidence in God is in direct proportion to our faith in him. As we listen to the stories of how God has come through for others, it increases our confidence that God will come through for us, too.

### SECTION THREE
# GOD'S GREATNESS

In order for God's goodness to be meaningful, he must also be great. A good God who is not also great may have wonderful intentions, but would be too weak to actually work on our behalf. When faced with the sin and darkness of this world, he would be easily defeated. In this section we'll see how God's goodness and his greatness are inextricably linked. We'll discover three central ways that God demonstrates his greatness and how each can increase our God-confidence.

## CHAPTER 9
# CREATION

I really like optical illusions. It fascinates me that the exact same scene, viewed from divergent perspectives, can appear vastly different. One of my favorite photographs is of two passenger jets on final approach at San Francisco International Airport. In the picture, it looks like the plane in the foreground is within a few feet of the plane just behind it. Surely they will both crash. In reality, the two planes were more than 650 feet apart, a normal and safe distance as each plane landed on its own runway. Perspective is everything.

Often, a person's background and experiences will lead them to see God primarily from one angle. But, in order to really know him, it's important that we understand him from all the various perspectives God gives us in Scripture. Imagine a beach ball, with each stripe a different color. When we live life predominantly on one stripe we see God as monochromatic. Perhaps you live on the justice stripe. You experience God as the color of justice. This leads you to believe that God is ultimately concerned with justice, so you better always do what's right. Obedience is everything. Someone else may live on the love stripe. They only see God as loving, merciful, and forgiving. This leads them to believe that it doesn't really matter what anybody does as long as they are sincere. After all, God only loves everybody. It's easy to see that our view of God, and therefore our view of life, can get really screwed up if we don't get the whole picture. God has all of these different stripes. He is just, but he's also loving. He is righteous, and he is forgiving. The Bible shows God to be all of these. We need to widen our perspective in order to understand God for who he really is and not simply for who we've imagined him to be.

A good God who isn't also great is easily overcome by evil. If God is a kindly old grandfather who just wants to spoil his grandkids, he may seem good, but he won't have your back when you're in a jam. He can't really protect you or provide for you. In fact, this view of God really reduces him to the level of a cosmic vending machine dispensing treats. In order for the good God to be able to apply his goodness, he must also be great. Otherwise, he is easily overcome by those forces who don't want to see good in this world.

On the other hand, a great God who isn't also good would be frightening. One day he may choose to be good, another day he may choose to be evil. He's capricious. You never know when you get up in the morning what kind of mood he'll be in.

The God of the Bible is both good and great. He is the most loving, gracious, and compassionate being in the universe, and he's also the most powerful one. His power ensures that he can exercise his love, grace, and compassion regardless of what evil may try to restrict him.

As I mentioned earlier, it's easier for me to believe that God is great than that he is good. We started with God's goodness, because if we don't believe that God's greatness is good for us, it won't help us in our confidence. In fact, it will have the opposite effect. We won't be confident that he wants to do good to us. Instead we'll always be waiting for the other shoe to drop. Knowing that God is good means we understand that he uses his greatness on our behalf. There are three realms, or three arenas in which God demonstrates his greatness. We can grow in God-confidence by grasping these three realms.

## THE PHYSICAL REALM

We spend most of our time interacting in the physical realm. This is the created world that we can experience through our senses. We understand it by what we can touch, taste, see, hear, and smell. Though he, himself, isn't a physical being, God also interacts with his creation. He is greater than anything in the physical realm.

Many of the challenges we face in life result from a problem in the physical realm. Weather is an example. You can touch the rain or snow. We can observe the barometric pressure changing. Tornadoes, hurricanes, floods, blizzards, and drought are all in the physical realm. Sickness and disease are in the physical realm. Airplanes, spiders, and heights are in the physical realm. Fires, earthquakes, and physical violence are all in the physical realm. God is greater than any of these.

What does God's greatness really mean? I know God is great, but sometimes it can seem pretty abstract. A synonym for greatness is power. If God is great, he is powerful. Power can be measured by that which is within its control. One way to think about God's greatness is in terms of what is under his control. In an earlier chapter we talked about the way God provides every breath that we breathe. He ensures that the air around us is just the right mix of oxygen, nitrogen, argon, carbon dioxide, and methane. God is great enough to do that everywhere on the planet, maybe on other planets for all we know. It's under his control.

## CONTROL

People like to talk about control as if we can maintain it. However, if you have kids or if you've ever babysat, or taught a Sunday school class, or if you manage people at work, then you know that human control is really just an illusion. We like to think we're in control of what happens, but we're really not. If little Jimmy wants to bolt right out of Sunday school and head for the nearest candy store, there's little you can do about it. If your team at work decides to mutiny and demand their own way, you'll discover just how limited your span of control really is. You can influence, you can beg and plead and cajole. You can order and threaten, but there are some things that are just beyond our ability to control.

That's why it's so amazing to realize that every single created thing is within God's control. The universe is so vast that even with the aid of modern technology we can't see it all. The building blocks of matter are so small we can hardly imagine them. People were fascinated in 1800 when John Dalton provided evidence that atoms existed. They were amazed in 1911 when Ernest Rutherford discovered that atoms have a nucleus. They were awestruck in 1968 when the Stanford Linear Accelerator Center definitively proved the existence of quarks. But God drew up the blueprints for all this eons ago, before he ever spoke creation into existence. He controls every speck of every quark (or whatever we go on to discover is even smaller than that) in existence.

Let's imagine that you are going to buy a computer. After doing some research, you've concluded that the most important factor in your buying decision is the level of customer service offered by the store. You want to shop at a place where they're going to know you by name, discern your individual needs, and understand the capabilities of the machines they have to offer. With this in mind, would you choose to shop at a large global chain for your computer or would you choose a little storefront owned by someone who has dedicated their life to selling and servicing computers? If your most important need is customer service, you will go to the smaller store. Why? Because the bigger something gets, the less we have control over each piece. We see this in all kinds of organizations. A company starts out with a fanatical focus on pleasing its customers, but as it grows and develops, it becomes impossible to maintain the same level of service. The company can create all kinds of rules and policies. They can try to deploy their best people to the most crucial places, but the fact remains that the bigger it gets, the less actual control they have over how front-line, customer-facing employees act.

God's level of control is not affected, however, by the vastness of his creation. God has control over the entire universe at its maximum macro meta scale, and still maintains equal control over the teeny tiny little quantum scale. God is in control of everything, the biggest, the smallest, and everything in between. That's true power, and only God is that great.

## IT'S NOTHING

Interestingly, as humans we often think of power and greatness in terms of destruction. Jason Bourne, the character of spy novels and action movies, is powerful because he can kill you twelve different ways with his bare hands. Russia is a powerful country because their nuclear arsenal can destroy vast swaths of human existence. The sun is powerful because its heat can fry an egg on the sidewalk even when blazing through the earth's protective atmosphere.

God's greatness isn't just demonstrated in that he controls everything that exists. He is so great that he created absolutely everything from absolutely nothing. Let that boggle your mind for a bit. He is in a category completely by himself. One to which we could never hope to attain.

People sometimes tell me I'm a creative person. I'm an author and speaker. I develop new ways of thinking about life and ministry. I'm also a musician. I write songs and record albums. It's a nice compliment to be thought of as creative, but everything I've ever created was really just a rearrangement of items that already existed. When I compose music, I don't invent new notes out of thin air.

The notes already exist in the universe. Certain vibrations sound at certain pitches because that's how God designed creation. All I do is arrange what has already been created into a (hopefully) pleasing series of organized sounds. I cannot create something from nothing. No one but God can do that.

> *Rejoice in the Lord always; again I will say, rejoice. Let your reasonableness be known to everyone. The Lord is at hand; do not be anxious about anything, but in everything by prayer and supplication with thanksgiving let your requests be made known to God. And the peace of God, which surpasses all understanding, will guard your hearts and your minds in Christ Jesus.*
> *(Philippians 4:4-7)*

God is greater than anything in the physical realm. He created it. Sin broke it. One day he'll renew it. We can be absolutely, totally confident in God because he has absolute, total control of every situation. He invites us to present our requests to him. He says that in doing so, we'll be relieved of our anxiety, fear, and worry. Notice what he says is the first part of the cure for anxiety: Rejoicing. When your anxiety is about the physical world, worship God for his creation and for his powerful greatness over everything that exists. If you're anxious about the thunderstorm, the doctor's report, the airplane trip, the crime rate, or anything else that is part of this physical realm, remind yourself that he is greater. Then, based on the faith and the confidence that he gives you, pray. Submit your requests to him. Ask him to move in your heart and in your circumstances. As you pray, know that he has promised to hear you and to take care of you (Matthew 5). You can be confident in God because he's greater than anything in the physical realm.

## CHAPTER 10

## SALVATION

I was away on a retreat recently, and at the end of the day I called my wife, Kathy.

"Merry misses you," she said.

"Aw, that's sweet," I replied.

"Say something to her," Kathy suggested.

Now at this point it's important for you, the reader, to know that our family has two cats, Pippin and Merry, named after two of the hobbits from Lord of the Rings, our daughter's favorite books. For some reason Merry has become my shadow, my buddy. She follows me around the house, wants me to pet her all the time, and complains when I'm not at home in the evenings. Still, what do you say to a cat, on the phone?

Both cats are indoor cats. They've never been outside. All they know is what exists within the four walls of the house and the bit of the outside world they can view from sitting in the window sills. There was no way for Merry to understand (if I had bothered to try to explain it) that I was at a hotel in another part of the state, that I was doing important work on this retreat, and that the work I did when I was away helped pay for her food and vet bills. Nor could she comprehend that I'd be home in a few days. In her tiny cat's mind, I was just gone, possibly never to be seen again.

Though we are most aware of the physical world we live in—that which we can see, hear, touch, taste, and smell—humans are also spiritual beings. Behind this physical realm is a spiritual world that we also interact with, and that affects the physical world of creation. Somewhat like Merry, the cat's experience of living in the house, yet being directly affected by forces outside the house which she is mostly unaware of, we live in a physical realm and are mostly unaware of the forces in the spiritual realm which impact us. The spiritual realm is just as real as the physical one, and is inhabited by God and spiritual beings like angels and demons.[6]

In the same way that God is greater than anything in the physical world, he is also greater than anything in the spiritual world. The actions he took in accomplishing our salvation show just how much greater God is than anything or anyone in the spiritual realm.

Think about this. Jesus lived a perfect life. (That, in and of itself, is testimony to God's triumph over the evil forces that exist to tempt and accuse us.) Then he went to the cross. On the third day, he was raised from the dead. Later he ascended to heaven. Each of these actions was accomplished in the face of bitter spiritual warfare.

The Bible gives us one glimpse into the intense spiritual warfare Jesus faced during his earthly life when it show us how the devil came and tempted him in the wilderness.

> *And Jesus, full of the Holy Spirit, returned from the Jordan and was led by the Spirit in the wilderness for forty days, being tempted by the devil. And he ate nothing during those days. And when they were ended, he was hungry. The devil said to him, "If you are the Son of God, command this stone to become bread." And Jesus answered him, "It is written, 'Man shall not live by bread alone.'" And the devil took him up and showed him all the kingdoms of the world in a moment of time, and said to him, "To you I will give all this authority and their glory, for it has been delivered to me, and I give it to whom I will. If you, then, will worship me, it will all be yours." And Jesus answered him, "It is written, "You shall worship the Lord your God, and him only shall you serve.'" And he took him to Jerusalem and set him on the pinnacle of the temple and said to him, "If you are the Son of God, throw yourself down from here, for it is written, "He will command his angels concerning you, to guard you,' and "On their hands they will bear you up, lest you strike your foot against a stone."' And Jesus answered him, "It is said, 'You shall not put the Lord your God to the test.'" And when the devil had ended every temptation, he departed from him until an opportune time. (Luke 4:1-13)*

Jesus is already physically weak when the devil shows up. Then, he's fighting for his life as the enemy hits him with issues around his identity, his calling, and his destiny. These temptations were very real and really hardcore. When they end, Luke tells us the devil left, but only until another opportunity came to tempt Jesus some more. During Jesus' 33 years or more on this planet, we can safely assume he faced pretty regular, very intense temptation. After all, if the devil could have enticed Jesus to sin, then it would have been all over, right? The enemy wins. Jesus is no longer the perfect lamb of God and salvation is impossible.

Some will say that it wasn't even possible for Jesus to have sinned because he is God, but the Bible says Jesus faced temptation just like we do (Hebrews 4:15). He didn't face life as a human until there was some difficulty and then just dip into his divine super powers. No, while he remained fully God and fully human, he faced life just as we do, as a human.

At the end of a life dogged by the devil, battling every temptation that is common to humans, he faces the cross. Jesus went willingly to the cross. He wasn't forced. We know it was incredibly difficult, not just physically, but emotionally and spiritually.

> *And he came out and went, as was his custom, to the Mount of Olives, and the disciples followed him. And when he came to the place, he said to them, "Pray that you may not enter into temptation." And he withdrew from them about a stone's throw, and knelt down and prayed, saying, "Father, if you are willing, remove this cup from me. Nevertheless, not my will, but yours, be done." And there appeared to him an angel from heaven, strengthening him. And being in agony he prayed more*

## SALVATION

*earnestly; and his sweat became like great drops of blood falling down to the ground. (Luke 22:39-44)*

In a time when we wear crosses around our necks as jewelry, it's easy to forget the horrors involved in being killed this way. Crucifixion was one of the most brutal and most shameful ways to die. It was preceded by hours of torture and was carried out publicly. Those punished in this way were hung on the cross for all to see as examples of what will happen to the worst of criminals.

Jesus understood exactly what he faced, and he longed for there to be another way. Still, knowing there wasn't, he willingly took the punishment that we deserved. Hanging between heaven and earth, he suffered the immense physical pain of this barbarous means of death. He experienced the intense emotional pain of being abandoned by his Heavenly Father (Mark 15:34). He took on the spiritual pain of becoming the sacrifice for the sin of the world. I can only imagine that at this point, the devil thought he had won. The Son of God lay in a cold tomb, dead, buried, and done. But then. Oh, but then, on the third day the greatest miracle of all occurs. Jesus' body no longer lies, cold and lifeless, in a rough stone grave. It wasn't misplaced. It wasn't moved. It wasn't stolen. He was raised from the dead, never to die again. Jesus is alive!

From the words the devil used when he tempted Jesus, and from the way the demons spoke to Jesus before he cast them out of people we know that the devil clearly understood who Jesus was. There's no question about that. If I'm the devil, and I understand who Jesus is, and I see him lying dead in the tomb, what's the one thing in the entire universe I will focus all my power to prevent? Jesus' resurrection. I'm going to dispatch every demon, evil spirit, power, and principality at my disposal to keep him in the ground. The whole game is on the line here. On this one moment, the entirety of history and the future of all things rest. What happens? In a most amazing, lopsided, blowout, God wins. All the powers of evil couldn't hold Jesus in the tomb. God is greater than anything and anyone in the spiritual realm. Period.

## LET'S MAKE IT INTERESTING

In the movie *Argo*, Ben Affleck plays real life CIA officer Antonio Mendez. In 1980 Mendez led the rescue of six United States diplomats from Iran during the 1979-1981 Iran hostage crisis. The movie details the true story of how Mendez created a fictional film company, snuck into Iran, and covertly escorted the diplomats to safety. It's truly an amazing story. But let's make it a bit more interesting.

What if Jimmy Carter, the President of the United States at the time, had called a press conference in the White House rose garden? Let's imagine that he announces to the gathering of international media that the Central Intelligence Agency was developing a plan to rescue these six diplomats. The plan involves entering Iranian airspace via plane, landing at Tehran International Airport, and traveling to a certain location where the American citizens are currently hiding. Once the CIA operative has met with them, he will lead them back through the airport to the plane and they'll fly right out of there. What would have happened? Do you think the Iranians would have responded to the circumstances somewhat differently? Might there have been more opposition?

For thousands of years before Jesus came, God revealed how the Messiah would come and set his people free from death and sin. The devil knew exactly what he was up against. He knew who Jesus was. He knew what was at stake and he mobilized every resource at his disposal to stop it. God wasn't just the winner on this one day in history. He didn't merely squeak out a victory over the forces of evil. He announced it beforehand, again and again. He said, "I'm taking on all contenders. I'm the biggest and the baddest, and I'm more powerful than anything the spiritual realm has ever seen. You better be ready to rumble!" But, they weren't. Not really. There was no way they could be when they were pitted against the LORD of Hosts, the Alpha and Omega, the King of kings and Lord of lords. God is greater.

Here's one more thing to think about. God didn't simply raise Jesus' body to life and bring him to heaven. When he was performing this tremendous, history-changing, destiny-altering miracle, he was also raising us from our spiritual death and exalting us to the highest place along with Jesus. Though we live on this physical planet and though one day our bodies will perish, in some mysterious way, we are seated on the throne with Christ at the right hand of our Heavenly Father. Don't believe me? Try this on for size:

> *But God, being rich in mercy, because of the great love with which he loved us, even when we were dead in our trespasses, made us alive together with Christ—by*

*grace you have been saved—and raised us up with him and seated us with him in the heavenly places in Christ Jesus. (Ephesians 2:4-6)*

Wow. The next time you feel scared, overwhelmed, stressed out, or insecure, remember where you are and what it took to get you there. God is great beyond measure and he has already, and will continue to, use that greatness on your behalf.

## THINKING IN CIRCLES

When it comes to fear, concern, worry, and insecurity, we live in two circles.[7] One is the circle of concern. The circle of concern is large. Included in the circle of concern is every single thing that might bear upon your existence. It may include your mother's health, your child's big test, peace in the Middle East, an upcoming election, global climate change, the economy, the spiritual journey your neighbors are on, the financial health of the company you work for, and on and on. It's a really big circle.

Inside the circle of concern is a much smaller circle, the circle of influence. The circle of influence includes only those issues you can realistically do something about. These are matters which I have the power to personally influence in some way.[8] My circle of influence might include ensuring that I am consistent and faithful at my job, making wise choices about how I spend my money, voting my conscience, recycling, sharing my faith with my neighbors, and so on.

It's vitally important that we distinguish between the circle of concern and the circle of influence. Many of us spend an inordinate amount of time thinking, fretting, and worrying about issues over which we have no influence. That takes away emotional energy we need to be able to focus on the matters we can actually do something about. There's an incredible sense of freedom in realizing that I can pray for what's in my circle of concern and then leave the results to God. I don't need to spend any more time engaging with them. It frees me to focus on those things I can change through my own actions.

When you're concerned, worried, anxious, fearful, scared or insecure ask yourself, "Does this fit into my circle of concern or my circle of influence? The jerk who's tailgating me fits into the circle of concern but not influence. (Unless I have really good insurance and I just want to jam on the brakes.) The local teachers' strike likely fits into my circle of concern, but not my circle of influence. The doctor's report on my mom's health fits into my circle of concern, but there's not a lot I can do personally to heal her cancer.

However, here's the cool thing: God's circle of influence and his circle of concern are both the same size. Everything in your circle of concern, and mine, and everyone else in the whole universe is in his circle of influence. There are millions of issues we aren't even aware of because they're happening half a universe away. Only the aliens living on those distant planets know and are concerned about them. All of that is in God's circle of influence. God's way bigger and more powerful than anything else in the spiritual realm.

## GROWING IN GOD-CONFIDENCE

When your anxiety is spiritual, emotional, or relational,

worship God for his victory. If you're depressed, worship God for his victory. If you're sad, worship God for his victory. Why? When you worship God for his victory, you are telling yourself the true story about who God is and what he's doing. It's a very different story than the one our hearts naturally believe. Our hearts naturally believe the story of our senses, what we can see, hear, smell, taste, and touch, but that is only part of the story. When we worship God for who he is, what he's said, and what he's done, we are telling ourselves the story as God tells it. We understand that he is the most powerful being in the universe and that he wants to use that power on our behalf. When we worship God, we're rehearsing the victory that he's already accomplished in Christ, which gives us confidence that he may want to do other things for us.

*What then shall we say to these things? If God is for us, who can be against us? He who did not spare his own Son but gave him up for us all, how will he not also with him graciously give us all things? (Romans 8:31-32)*

God gave us Jesus. Won't he also give us peace, joy, comfort, love, patience, kindness, boldness, courage, wisdom, and any other thing that we need? Won't he also work all these things together for our good? Of course he will.

We can be confident in him because he's good, he's powerful, and nothing will stand in his way. He takes it seriously when you face hardship, persecution, sickness, loneliness, and sadness. He understands when you've been hurt or wronged, when you've lost a loved one or seen a dream snuffed out. He knows what it's like to grieve and to suffer rejection. Best of all, he's good and great enough to help you through it.

> *Oh come, let us sing to the LORD; let us make a joyful noise to the rock of our salvation! Let us come into his presence with thanksgiving; let us make a joyful noise to him with songs of praise! For the LORD is a great God, and a great King above all gods. In his hand are the depths of the earth; the heights of the mountains are his also. ... Oh come, let us worship and bow down; let us kneel before the LORD, our Maker! For he is our God, and we are the people of his pasture, and the sheep of his hand. Today, if you hear his voice, (Psalm 95:1-4, 6-7)*

Once you've worshiped God for his victory, you can appropriate that victory for yourself. In his second letter to Timothy, Paul says that, "God gave us a spirit not of fear but of power and love and self-control (2 Timothy 1:7)."

Probably the best translation I've heard of the word fear in that verse is "woozy-ness." Rather than being woozy—foggy-headed, confused, unsure, and powerless—we can have clarity, wisdom, love and power. As we worship God we apply those truths about God to our situation. We say, "God I praise you because you are a solid rock that cannot be moved. My foundation is in you. Father, I take my stand on you and your Word right now. You have promised that those who trust in you will never be put to shame. I've been worried about this issue and I refuse to allow it to control me any longer. I recognize that you are greater than what

I'm facing right now and I choose to revere you more than this other concern. I stand firm on the truth that you are great and you are good and you love me and that you want to use your goodness and greatness on my behalf. I claim the peace of God that transcends all understanding and rest in your loving arms. In Jesus' name. Amen."

## CHAPTER 11
## DECLARATION

How about a little discussion on physics? The physical realm that we interact with through our senses contains three dimensions: length, width, and depth. We are comfortable with these dimensions, having engaged with them every day of our lives. We utilize them every time we color with crayons, plan how to furnish a room, or drive a car. The Bible is quite mum on the subject of how many dimensions the spiritual realm has. I imagine it as much like the physical realm only with brighter colors. Oh, and you can walk through walls, disappear, fly, and other cool stuff. The fourth dimension is time. In some way, the three dimensions of the physical realm (and possibly the dimensions of the spiritual realm) experience time in a logical sequence.[9]

We've seen that God is greater than anything in the physical and spiritual realms. Now let's look at God's greatness in the temporal realm. God is greater than anything in time. No matter the length of time between God's promise and his action, nothing can stop it, modify it, delay it or rush it. It will happen in just the right way, with just the right people, at just the right moment. God's promises will come through. They may take 700 years, but his purposes will prevail and the timing will be perfect.

Throughout Scripture we see God working in a kind of rhythm where he gives us assurance, then he provides deliverance, and then he exhorts us to remembrance. Assurance, deliverance, remembrance. The cycle appears at a macro level that begins in Genesis and ends in the New Testament. Once you discover it, you begin to see it all over the Bible at different levels.

## THE OLD TESTAMENT PATTERN

In Genesis chapter 15, God promises to make Abraham (then still known as Abram) into a great nation. Abram is struggling to believe God, so God takes him outside and tells him to look at all the stars in the sky. In Chicago, where I live, we never see the stars because the city is so bright it drowns out the light of the stars, but in the time and place Abram lived there was nothing to keep the light of every star from shining brightly at night. God says, 'Look at the sky. Try counting all those stars. That's how many descendants I'm going to give you." God makes an audacious promise to Abram, assuring him that he will make him a great nation and give his descendants the land on which he is now living (Genesis 15:5-21).

Moving forward in time, we read in Exodus chapter 14 about how God rescues Israel (Abraham's descendants) from slavery in Egypt. He punishes the people of Egypt, brings his people out of their oppression, and in a final act of triumph, miraculously guides them through the Red Sea. God provides deliverance.

From the time God gave Abram assurance in Genesis 15 to the time he provided deliverance in Exodus 14 is three generations plus 400 years[10] or roughly 500 years or so. How long is 500 years? Well, just over 500 years ago Martin Luther nailed his 95 theses to the door of a church in Wittenberg and sparked the Protestant reformation. Five hundred years ago the United States wasn't even a dream. In fact, as of this writing, Columbus's famous trip to the Americas was 528 years ago. That's a long time between promise and fulfillment, right? Yet that's how God planned for it to go.

God gives assurance, then provides deliverance, and he asks us to regularly remember that he kept his promise. The night God rescued his people from Egypt he instituted a ceremonial meal called the Passover, designed to help his people remember their great deliverance throughout the generations. (This should sound familiar. What we call The Lord's Supper was a Passover meal. Jesus infused it with new meaning for Christians and we are to regularly celebrate it in remembrance of him.) God passed through the land of Egypt, killing all the firstborn sons, but he "passed over" and didn't kill the firstborn of Israel (Exodus 12:1-29). This led Pharaoh, king of Egypt, to finally set Israel free. Once they were through the Red Sea, God said this to Moses:

> *And the LORD spoke to Moses in the wilderness of Sinai, in the first month of the second year after they had come out of the land of Egypt, saying, "Let the people of*

> *Israel keep the Passover at its appointed time. On the fourteenth day of this month, at twilight, you shall keep it at its appointed time; according to all its statutes and all its rules you shall keep it." So Moses told the people of Israel that they should keep the Passover. And they kept the Passover in the first month, on the fourteenth day of the month, at twilight, in the wilderness of Sinai; according to all that the LORD commanded Moses, so the people of Israel did. (Numbers 9:1-5)*

Remembrance is essential. Humans are so forgetful. I can't even remember my cell phone when I leave for work. If I'm not careful, weeks, months, or even longer will go by without having spent any real time contemplating my deliverance in Christ. That's why these times of remembrance are so vitally important.

## THE NEW TESTAMENT PATTERN

In the New Testament we see this same pattern. In Genesis chapter three, just after Adam and Eve sinned, God makes a powerful declaration.

> *And I will put enmity between you and the woman, and between your offspring and hers; he will crush your head, and you will strike his heel." (Genesis 3:15 NIV)*

Though he is speaking to the serpent, he is making a promise to the humans. He declares his intent to one day destroy the evil represented by the serpent and his lies. This is assurance. God then repeats this assurance again and again in dozens of different ways. Take this example from the prophet Isaiah.

> *A voice cries: "In the wilderness prepare the way of the LORD; make straight in the desert a highway for our God. Every valley shall be lifted up, and every mountain and hill be made low; the uneven ground shall become level, and the rough places a plain. And the glory of the LORD shall be revealed, and all flesh shall see it together, for the mouth of the LORD has spoken." (Isaiah 40:3-5)*

These very words are used in the New Testament to describe John the Baptist's ministry as he prepared the way for Jesus.

> *In those days John the Baptist came preaching in the wilderness of Judea, "Repent, for the kingdom of heaven is at hand." For this is he who was spoken of by the prophet Isaiah when he said, "The voice of one crying in the wilderness: 'Prepare the way of the Lord; make his paths straight.'" (Matthew 3:1-3)*

This is God's way of pointing people back to his promise. "Hey, pay attention! Messiah is coming. Let me assure you, I'm on the move."

Fast forward to the crucifixion of Christ. By stirring up the people against him, the devil strikes the heel of Eve's offspring (Jesus) at the cross. But in a surprising reversal, Jesus, in his very death, crushes the head of the serpent (the devil). By dying, he attains victory over sin and death for all people. In the cross and resurrection, God makes good on his promise. He delivers us from the power and penalty of sin.

Right before Jesus goes to the cross, he institutes a ceremony of remembrance. This is how the apostle Paul describes it:

> *For I received from the Lord what I also delivered to you, that the Lord Jesus on the night when he was betrayed took bread, and when he had given thanks, he broke it, and said, "This is my body which is for you. Do this in remembrance of me." In the same way also he took the cup, after supper, saying, "This cup is the new covenant in my blood. Do this, as often as you drink it, in remembrance of me." For as often as you eat this bread and drink the cup, you proclaim the Lord's death until he comes. (1 Corinthians 11:23-26)*

We are to remember the deliverance bought for us by the blood of Christ. The arc is complete: assurance, deliverance, remembrance. Though modern believers often overlook or downplay it, the remembrance piece is incredibly important. It's as we participate in remembering our deliverance that our faith is built and we grow in confidence that God is both great and good and working on our behalf.

We don't know what year God made his promise to Adam and Eve, but from the time Isaiah prophesied until the time when Jesus actually came to take our sin on the cross was about 700 years. What happened 700 years ago from today? Maybe the most known-about historic event from 700 years ago is the bubonic plague. This was before Michelangelo, Da Vinci, or Columbus and right after Marco Polo. That's a very, very long time to have faith.

## THE IMPORTANCE OF REMEMBERING

> *Therefore, since we are surrounded by so great a cloud of witnesses, let us also lay aside every weight, and sin which clings so closely, and let us run with endurance the race that is set before us, looking to Jesus, the founder and perfecter of our faith, who for the joy that was set before him endured the cross, despising the shame, and is seated at the right hand of the throne of God. Consider him who endured from sinners such hostility against himself, so that you may not grow weary or fainthearted.*
> *(Hebrews 12:1-3)*

Remembering the great cloud of witnesses who went before us, whose lives testify to the goodness of God, motivates us to lay aside the sin which prevents us from running the race of life effectively. Remembering Jesus, his actions and what he suffered, gives us the endurance we need to persevere in times of trouble. Remembering gives us clarity, courage, strength, and determination when we most need it.

What's the point of the Lord's Supper? It is to remember all that Jesus accomplished for us. It is to proclaim to ourselves, one another, and the watching world, that his death was not meaningless, though its full impact has yet to be felt. It is to increase our faith that one day Christ will return and complete our deliverance from sin. We have been delivered from its punishment and its power, but we still live with its presence. The day is coming that all the effects of sin will be reversed and we will be completely redeemed and free.

Assurance, deliverance, remembrance. God is greater than anything in the temporal world. When we remember the powerful acts of God throughout Scripture and in history, it builds our faith for what God can do in our present situation.

As I have been writing this book, I have been thinking about times when God has worked in power throughout history, throughout Scripture, throughout the lives of people I know, and I have been praying, "God, please do that. We need that. We need to be more confident in you. We need a stronger, more robust, healthy, Arnold Schwarzenegger-esque faith. God, please do this. I know you can transform us, because it's what you've done in the past." To be honest, I don't pray that way often enough. What would our prayer lives be like if we always prayed with that kind of confidence? What if we always prayed in light of the fact that God has power over everything in the physical realm, the spiritual realm, the temporal realm and he wants to use that power on our behalf?

## WHEN TO WORK AND WHEN TO WAIT

This raises a practical question for us, however. When do we work and when do we wait? When do we simply trust that God will move on his own timetable, and when do we work with all our energy to make something happen?

When my wife and I bought our first house, there was

a problem with our loan application. Even though there were a number of reasons we should have been slam dunk borrowers, banks were not interested in us. Although our broker was very good and he was working very hard, we just couldn't get things approved.

I was driving home from work one day in the middle of this frustrating season, and the idea came to me that maybe this wasn't a financial issue. We had done everything we knew how to do financially. We'd filled out the right forms, made the right arguments. Applied to the right places. People who knew about these things couldn't figure out why we kept being rejected. Could there be something else going on here? The more time went by, the more pressure we were under. If we couldn't get a loan in time, we weren't going to get the house.

We faced the very real question, "Do we continue to work with our broker, applying to the ever-smaller list of potential lenders? Or do we stop and take a breath?" Maybe God wanted to do something that we didn't understand. So we stopped. We waited. We prayed. We prayed in a different way than we had been praying. Rather than asking God to give us favor with the bank, we began asking God to break through whatever was blocking us from receiving a loan. In less than a week, we had a loan and we got the house.

Is there a chance this was coincidence? Of course. But, I don't think it was. I think something was happening in the spiritual realm, and God wanted us to be still, and focus more on him than on the bank. Now please don't read this and think I'm Mr. Super-spiritual-discernment-man. I'm not. This is simply an example of a time when the right thing to do was wait and pray rather than try to figure it out and work harder. How do you know which to do? When is it right to work the problem and when is waiting on the Lord the right thing to do?

## I'M NOT SURE THAT WORD MEANS WHAT YOU THINK IT MEANS

Before we can decide when to wait, we need to agree on exactly what we mean by the word. Most people are probably familiar with the famous passage in Isaiah that talks about waiting on the LORD. In the English Standard Version of the Bible it reads like this.

> *Even youths shall faint and be weary, and young men shall fall exhausted; but they who wait for the LORD shall renew their strength; they shall mount up with wings like eagles; they shall run and not be weary; they shall walk and not faint. (Isaiah 40:30-31)*

I like the English Standard translation of Scripture. It follows the original Hebrew and Greek text very closely, which is one of the reasons most of the Bible verses quoted in this book use that translation. But in this case, using the word "wait" in verse 31 may lead to some confusion. The old King James Version also used the word wait here, but the Hebrew word doesn't mean quite the same thing that comes to modern English-speakers' minds when we hear the word. When someone tells us to wait, the most natural response is to stop what we're doing. Implied in its everyday usage is the idea that we cease our activity. When my wife and I are out for a walk and she says, "Wait for me," she means that I should stop walking until she catches up. She doesn't mean that I should keep walking and she'll run to make up the ground and then we'll continue on together.

The Hebrew word in this context probably means something more like "confident expectation." Rather than God saying, "Those that stop what they are doing and wait for God to move will renew their strength," he is actually saying something more like, "Those who confidently expect God to move, they will renew their strength."

## IT'S NOT WORKING

Several years ago I was scheduled to play drums at church. I'm not much of a morning person anyway, but that particular Sunday I woke up feeling like I'd been run over by a truck. I was totally beat. Being a pastor and a good Christian, I decided I was gonna take God at his word and wait on the Lord. So I laid there in bed and waited ... and waited ... and waited, but the strength never came. I was still just as tired after hitting the snooze for the fourth time. Eventually I just got up anyway.

Arriving at church I discovered we were going to sing Chris Tomlin's song, "Everlasting." It begins with the words,

> Strength will rise as we wait upon the Lord
> As we wait upon the Lord
> As we wait upon the Lord.

I complained to the worship pastor. "Look, I've been waiting on the Lord all morning and my strength still isn't rising."

He laughed and replied, "John, you know darn well that's not what 'waiting on the Lord' means." He was right, but I still wanted to go back to sleep.

The phrase "wait on the Lord" doesn't mean "do nothing." If your hope and faith are in God, doing nothing in a given circumstance may be the right thing, but you can also "wait on the Lord" and be actively engaged. Where is your hope? In what, or whom, is your faith? From where do you get your courage? Who are you looking toward to solve this issue? Your answers to these questions will tell you if you're "waiting on the Lord." The first issue to resolve is where our hope is.

Let's imagine for a minute I have a large gallstone. It's been determined I need my gallbladder removed. I schedule the surgery. The doctor can't do it for six weeks. So I take matters into my own hands and decide to do it myself.

That's actually how many of the Christians I know operate. (See what I did there?) They have a problem. They pray about it. God doesn't seem to do anything. They take matters into their own hands. Then, a year later, two years later, or 10 years later, they regret it. You always regret it if you work simply because you got tired of trusting. God's timing is perfect.

Are you working because you're afraid God isn't working? Stop. Are you working because you just have to do something and you can't sit still? Stop. Clean the house, read a book, go see a ball game, go ahead and do something, just don't work the problem. Working on the problem has to be an act of faith just like waiting does. Otherwise your work is motivated by fear, not faith. Scripture says that whatever isn't the result of faith is sin (Romans 14:23). As long as you can work the problem in faith, great. Do that. But the minute you start to get desperate and it feels like, "Oh my gosh, if this doesn't work out, I'm totally lost." Stop. Maybe just for five minutes, maybe for five weeks. Stop until you can get your eyes back on Jesus and realize that God is in charge of the timing. Your decision to work or wait demonstrates what you believe about God and his power in the temporal realm. If you work from faith, it declares your trust in him. If you work from desperation, it declares your fear.

## TIMING IS EVERYTHING

A former colleague, we'll call her Sharon, worked at the front desk of an organization I led. Her responsibilities included answering phones, welcoming people, scheduling appointments, and often speaking in both English and Spanish depending on the needs of the people she was talking to. Almost from the day I started at this organization I sensed that there was more to this young woman than was immediately apparent. She was smart; she anticipated needs; she interacted with people really well, even in tense situations. As time went on, I discovered that she had a Masters degree in public policy. More and more, I began wondering why she was sitting at the front desk, answering our phones.

A few months after starting I had to hire someone for a strategic, director-level position in the organization. As a general rule, I prefer to hire from within an organization, or at least hire people whose track record I, or someone I trust, can vouch for. The more I thought about the needs of the position, the more I thought Sharon might be someone to consider. Her education was right, her demeanor was right, she was already sold on the mission and values of the organization.

When I asked a couple of the other directors on my leadership team about Sharon they said, "You know, she actually applied for that very role under your predecessor and was turned down." When I asked why she was turned down, nobody really knew. I asked Sharon if she wanted to apply for the role. She said she wasn't sure since she had applied in the past and been rejected, so I suggested we just meet to explore the possibility together. I would tell her what I'm looking for in the position. She could tell me if it sounded interesting and like something she would enjoy and be good at. We met. We talked. She was interested. I promoted her to the new role.

Do you know what she did? She absolutely transformed that role. She was amazing. She accomplished objectives in the role I had never considered. It turns out she is one of those people who just raises the bar on everything. It was fantastic. From my perspective, promoting her was a huge win. From her perspective, spending two years working a job for which she was highly over-qualified couldn't have been fun. In retrospect, she probably wouldn't have enjoyed the new role under the old leader because that person had a very different way of working than I did. Working with the new leadership team we were forming, building the kind of organization we both had a vision for, she really blossomed and has done great work for that organization. In the rear view mirror, God's timing is perfect, though it rarely looks that way through the windshield.

God is greater than anything in the temporal realm. The apostle Peter tells us that the Lord isn't slow in keeping his promises, though it's easy for us to feel that way. Rather, he is being patient because he doesn't want any to perish, but wants everyone to repent (2 Peter 3:9). In his letter to the Galatians Paul says it this way.

*And let us not grow weary of doing good, for in due season we will reap, if we do not give up. (Galatians 6:9)*

## GROWING IN GOD-CONFIDENCE

Sometimes we get anxious because our timing and God's timing don't match up. We need to patiently trust that God knows what he's doing. We don't have all the facts, and we can't seem to find clarity. When this happens we can worship God for his Word, especially for his promises and his historic faithfulness. Ask yourself how God came through in the past. What must it have felt like to those people between the time God assured them that he was going to do something and the time that he actually delivered them? How has it looked like he won't come through?

Read the stories of people like King Jehoshaphat. Three other nations joined forces and came to attack him. When he learned about it, his first response was to gather up all the people and hold a giant prayer meeting. I love what he prayed. He said. "God, we don't know what to do, but our eyes are on you." That's so honest and vulnerable. In front of all the people who looked to him for leadership he confessed that he had no idea what to do. At the same time, he knew God was powerful enough to do anything and so their hope and trust were in him.

When they finish praying, God promises he'll deliver them. They're so confident in God that they send the choir out in front of the military. I dunno what's up with that. Being a musician, I might be a little bit offended, but God destroys the enemy in front of them. They didn't even have to fight. All that remained was for them to gather up the spoils (2 Chronicles 2:1-30).

Jesus tells us in John 15:7-8 that if we will abide in him and if his words abide in us, we can ask whatever we want and it will be done for us. Then he says that this actually glorifies his father. Wow. The Heavenly Father is glorified when he does stuff for you. That's crazy, isn't it?

I often have a scarcity mentality when I pray. I feel like resources are scarce and people have more important needs than mine, so God really can't prioritize anything for me. Jesus straight out contradicts this. He says God is glorified when I bear much fruit, so I should ask for what I need.

*If you abide in me, and my words abide in you, ask whatever you wish, and it will be done for you. By this my Father is glorified, that you bear much fruit and so prove to be my disciples. As the Father has loved me, so have I loved you. Abide in my love. If you keep my commandments, you will abide in my love, just as I have kept my Father's commandments and abide in his love. These things I have spoken to you, that my joy may be in you, and that your joy may be full. (John 15:7-11)*

Read that last sentence again. How does Jesus want us to feel? Joyful! The whole point of what he has said to this point is that we may experience his joy to the fullest possible extent.

Jesus gives us three practical ways to begin experiencing his joy. First, soak in God's Word. The more you're in God's Word, the more you'll know how to ask for what God already wants to give. Second, ask God for what you need. The apostle James tells us that we don't have what we need because we don't ask for it (James 4:2). When we are saturated with God's Word we will ask for what God wants to give, and he gives it to us. Third, keep his commandments. Live within the framework of love that he has set out for us. Don't go running out of the yard and into the street when God's told you to stay in the yard. Though it may not seem like it to us, that's dangerous. When we do these three things: Soak in God's Word, ask for what we need, and live within his framework, we will find our jittery fear being replaced with joyful faith.

God is greater than anything in the temporal realm. He is greater than anything in the spiritual realm. He's greater than anything in the physical realm. Amazingly, he wants to use that greatness, he wants to use that power on your behalf.

SECTION 4

# PUTTING IT ALL TOGETHER

A colleague of mine used to coach NCAA Division III men's basketball. In thinking about how to make achieving God-confidence as practical as possible, it occurred to me that the process is similar to preparing a basketball team to win a big game.

In this section we'll start putting all the pieces together. What do we need to actually do in order to grow in God-confidence? If you have jumped to this section first (let's be honest, that's what I would do), I encourage you to take the time to go back and prayerfully read the first three sections before trying to put it all together. After all, without a deep understanding of the biblical principles, you won't be able to implement them in a way that truly brings transformation.

A companion to this book, *The God-confidence Playbook* is also available It greatly expands on this section and can be helpful in working out the details of the specific challenges you face.

## CHAPTER 12
## THE ESTATE

Before we start talking about basketball, lets circle back for a minute. We ended section three with the idea of obedience, or living within God's framework. If you're like me, you may have an aversion to the word obey. It's one of my least favorite words in the English lexicon. I think I may actually be allergic to it. When God says, "Obey," I want to say, "No way." When I think about obedience, I picture a slave on a Viking ship. Dressed in rags, he is manacled to the bench he shares with others laboring hard to keep the vessel moving. Standing above the benches, the ship's bosun cracks his whip over their heads. "Obey!" he shouts, and they have no choice but to do it.

When the Bible talks about obedience, it looks quite different. Imagine God has given you a 2,000 acre estate. It has forests, and hills, and a large, clear water lake. There is a gorgeous castle right in the middle of it. The castle's garage is filled with every kind of motorized toy and sports equipment you could want. All kinds of wildlife roam the estate, and a towering mountain range rises at its outskirts.

God says to you, "I have given you this entire estate to live on. Everything you need to be happy and fulfilled is here. The only thing I ask is that you stay on the ranch. Please don't leave the property, and especially don't go into the nearby mountains. They are very dangerous."

## FROM MAGNIFICENT TO MUNDANE

Now if you're like me, this is what you do: You start by exploring the grand castle. Then you check out the toys in the garage. You explore the woods and snorkel in the lake and enjoy the surprise of how tame the animals are on this grand estate. Pretty soon, though, you start to feel drawn to the great mountain range just off the estate. Eventually you take your state-of-the-art tent and pitch it on the very corner of the estate. You fill your days exploring the forbidden mountains, returning every night to sleep in the tent on your property. Over time, you look at your freeze dried food, your filtered water, and your dirty clothes and you wonder why God is such a grouchy old miser and horrible provider. You've forgotten all about the blessings and beauty God has graced you with.

God has given us this magnificent, wonderful life to live, but we so often ignore it to explore the dark underbelly of forbidden sin. Then we wonder why we struggle to experience God's love, joy, grace, and peace.

## THE FEAR OF WHAT IF

Your challenge may not be quite that straightforward. Maybe you have stayed on the estate, but still aren't experiencing the joy, peace, comfort, and boldness that God has promised. Often the enemy uses fear to keep us from life as it could be lived. You could be exploring and experiencing every wonderful inch of the blessings and grace of God. Instead, you're huddled in a corner afraid of what might be outside the light of your sputtering campfire. "What if...?" becomes your mantra. What if the bears find us? What if the wolves eat us? What if my plane crashes? What if it's cancer? What if the tooth falls out? What if she turns me down? What if the company folds? What if? What if? What if?

Pretty soon the fear keeps you from enjoying every part of the estate. You stop going into the woods because you're afraid of what animals might be in there. You stop swimming in the lake for fear that the water might contain bacteria. You stop going outside at all because everything just seems dangerous. Then you stop going upstairs because it seems spooky. You stop going in the kitchen because there are funny noises there. You stop leaving the bedroom because the floorboards in the halls creak. You stop getting out of bed because there might be monsters under there. Until eventually your entire life is lived on one tiny corner of the bed. That's the only place you feel safe. That's the enemy's plan. Nowhere feels safe.

If we only consider the physical reality, there's some truth to that. Nowhere on this planet is one hundred percent safe. The building you're in could collapse under you at any minute. Who knows? What if you get in the elevator and it crashes. You might back your car out of your driveway and get hit by a truck. You could be hit by a falling satellite while you're out jogging and be instantly crushed. You could spontaneously combust walking up your front steps. Unlikely, but anything can happen. That's exactly the point, right? Not just anything can happen. Only those events God has pre-approved are allowed into our lives.

As believers, we view life not from birth to death, but from birth to resurrection. The "worst" that could happen is we go home to an eternity of splendor and joy with Jesus. When we view life that way, we aren't nearly as concerned about things like spontaneous combustion, elevators crashing, crocodiles eating us, or spiders the size of a basketball biting us with their poisonous venom. (Yeah, there are reasons I'll never be a missionary in Africa, okay?) Don't allow the enemy to trick you into exploring sin because he's convinced you that God's a mean, ugly ogre. Don't allow the fear to push you into living on the corner of your bed because you're convinced everywhere else is too scary.

How do we get past the fear and the enemy?

The path to our deepest dreams runs through the forest of our greatest fears. Always. What has God put most deeply in your heart? What does he want to accomplish through you in this world? The path to that dream inevitably leads through the forest of your greatest fears. You will face your greatest fears or you will not accomplish your deepest dreams. That's just the way God wired the world. Why? Because he is most interested in your faith. The seven steps that make up the rest of this book can help you join God as he builds your shield of faith into a solid, robust, defense stronger than any fiery darts the enemy may shoot your way.

## CHAPTER 13

# ENSURE YOU UNDERSTAND THE GAME

First, we have to ensure we understand the game in which we live. We can't succeed, we can't win, if we don't know how the game is played. If you're coaching a basketball team, you need to understand that the way to win has nothing to do with hitting home runs (that's baseball) or kicking field goals (that's American football). The only way to win at basketball is to shoot the ball through the hoop.

> *For everyone who has been born of God overcomes the world. And this is the victory that has overcome the world—our faith. Who is it that overcomes the world except the one who believes that Jesus is the Son of God? (1 John 5:4-5)*

What is the victory? Our faith. Sadly, many believers spend much of their lives trying to win the wrong game. We think the most important thing is how little we swear, or how nice we are to people, or how much we speak out against the world, or how many Bible verses we know, or how little we associate with non-Christians. If you get nothing else from this book, I hope you understand this: It's all about faith. What God cares about most is your faith. Everything else in life rests on faith. All other actions and motivations are the natural result of faith. If you don't have faith, it doesn't matter how obedient you are. Just look at the Pharisees. Without faith, all the sincerity in the world is pointless, because without faith you can't please God (Hebrews 11:6).

If I'm a basketball player, my team can only win by scoring more points than the other team. We score those points by putting the ball through the hoop. There's no other way to score. We can play really hard, we can keep from committing any fouls, we can unselfishly pass the ball to our teammates, but unless we're shooting baskets we're going to lose.

So in the game of life, what scores points? Faith. In the book of 1 Corinthians Paul uses the analogy of building materials. What we build with gold, silver, and precious stones brings a reward. What we build with wood hay and straw gets burned up (1 Corinthians 3:11-15). Those things built of gold, silver, and precious stones last for eternity. They are the "treasures in heaven" that Jesus talks about (Matthew 6:20). It's impossible to lay up treasures in heaven, to build with gold, silver, and precious stones, without faith. It requires faith to give up the wood, hay, and straw of this world. It requires faith to invest in eternity rather than becoming comfortable in this broken, fallen, temporary realm. Your team can be the best at dribbling, passing, and defense, but if you can't score, you can't win. You can be the best at serving in the church, being a nice person, and giving all your money to missions, but if you don't have faith you'll still lose in the end. The apostle Paul says the only thing that counts is faith working through love (Galatians 5:6).

## THE REASON FOR FEAR

Little faith is the central reason we struggle with fear. We rarely see Jesus bemoaning disobedience in the gospels. Rather we often hear him commenting on the size of people's faith (Matthew 6:30; 8:26; 14:31; 16:8; and 17:20). "Oh, you of little faith." It's for this reason that a strong relationship built with Jesus before the moment of fear is vital. Because when you're in that moment, facing something scary, it's too late. If I'm gripping the armrests of the airplane, and I'm sure we're going to crash and die, and I'm sweating bullets, it's too late to build my faith. My faith needs to be built in preparation for that moment.

So, how do you win? Grow your faith.

## CHAPTER 14

# WATCH GAME TAPE

Once we are sure we understand the game in general, we begin to focus on the specific team we'll be facing. We do this by watching game tape. (I'm aware that actual video tape isn't used anymore, but they still call it this.) If I'm preparing to coach my team, I need a game plan. If I want to ensure that my game plan is effective, I need to understand the other team, so I watch game tape of the other team in action. By doing this I begin to see patterns in how the opposition plays. I see what other teams have done to defeat them. Game tapes show the historical record of what's been tried, what's failed, and what's succeeded. They give me vital information for my own encounter with the opposing team.

For our purposes, watching game tape equates to immersing ourselves in Scripture. As we see how others have grown in their faith, we can adopt their winning strategies. As we read the letters of winning coaches who have gone before us, we can heed their warnings, embrace their exhortations, and follow their examples. Our game plan may look great on paper, but if it's not rooted in the tactics that have proven to win in the past, they're probably just a fantasy. In the same way, if the internal beliefs of our hearts and minds aren't built solidly on the truths of Scripture, our faith rests on vapor, like castles in the clouds.

## THE THEREFORE

Whole books have been written on how to study Scripture. We certainly don't have space here to explore the many great ways of hearing from God through his Word, but let me point out one simple, yet powerful, observation that can change how we understand and apply the Bible. It involves noticing the single word: "therefore."

Unless you're an attorney or a pastor, you probably don't utilize the word therefore in everyday speech. It's popularity has waned in recent years, but the Bible uses the word quite a bit and it serves an important purpose. Let's start with an example from the book of Genesis.

> *It is as I told Pharaoh; God has shown to Pharaoh what he is about to do. There will come seven years of great plenty throughout all the land of Egypt, but after them there will arise seven years of famine, and all the plenty will be forgotten in the land of Egypt. The famine will consume the land, and the plenty will be unknown in the land by reason of the famine that will follow, for it will be very severe. And the doubling of Pharaoh's dream means that the thing is fixed by God, and God will shortly bring it about. Now* therefore *let Pharaoh select*

*a discerning and wise man, and set him over the land of Egypt. (Genesis 41:28-33 emphasis added)*

In this Old Testament passage Joseph is interpreting two dreams of Pharaoh, king of Egypt. In the last sentence of the passage Joseph moves from directly interpreting what was in the dreams to giving some advice to Pharaoh about what to do in response to the dreams. He makes this verbal transition using the words, "Now, therefore." In doing so, he is showing that what follows the word "therefore" is based on what came before it. One old preacher used to say, "Whenever you see the word 'therefore' you need to look to see what it's there for." In this passage Joseph is showing us that his advice to Pharaoh about what he should do is based on the interpretation of the dreams God gave him. To the degree that he has correctly interpreted Pharaoh's dreams, the advice will be valuable. Let's look at another example.

*It was not because you were more in number than any other people that the LORD set his love on you and chose you, for you were the fewest of all peoples, but it is because the LORD loves you and is keeping the oath that he swore to your fathers, that the LORD has brought you out with a mighty hand and redeemed you from the house of slavery, from the hand of Pharaoh king of Egypt. Know* therefore *that the LORD your God is God, the faithful God who keeps covenant and steadfast love with those who love him and keep his commandments, to a thousand generations, and repays to their face those who hate him, by destroying them. He will not be slack*

> with one who hates him. He will repay him to his face. (Deuteronomy 7:7-10 emphasis added)

Here God is giving his law to the people of Israel in the wilderness. He explains that he didn't choose them to be his people because they were great and wonderful, but rather because of his own love and the promise that he made to their forefathers, Abraham, Isaac, and Jacob. He then says, "Know therefore that the LORD your God is God ..." The second half of the passage is built on the first. They can know, remember, and build their lives on the truth that God is faithful, loving, and just because he demonstrated those qualities already. One way to think of it is to substitute, "For this reason" for the word "therefore." Let's look at a couple New Testament passages and then we'll make this really practical.

> I tell you this, brothers: flesh and blood cannot inherit the kingdom of God, nor does the perishable inherit the imperishable. Behold! I tell you a mystery. We shall not all sleep, but we shall all be changed, in a moment, in the twinkling of an eye, at the last trumpet. For the trumpet will sound, and the dead will be raised imperishable, and we shall be changed. For this perishable body must put on the imperishable, and this mortal body must put on immortality. When the perishable puts on the imperishable, and the mortal puts on immortality, then shall come to pass the saying that is written: "Death is swallowed up in victory." "O death, where is your victory? O death, where is your sting?" The sting of death

*is sin, and the power of sin is the law. But thanks be to God, who gives us the victory through our Lord Jesus Christ.* Therefore, *my beloved brothers, be steadfast, immovable, always abounding in the work of the Lord, knowing that in the Lord your labor is not in vain.*
*(1 Corinthians 15:50-58 emphasis added)*

In this wonderful passage on Christ's victory over sin and death, Paul explains what will happen in the last days when God "gives us the victory through our Lord Jesus Christ." Then Paul pivots to make a new point, that we should be steadfast, immovable, and laboring for God's Kingdom. He makes this verbal pivot by using the word "therefore." The reason we can be steadfast and immovable is that God, in Christ, is giving us the victory over sin and death. The exhortation for our action rests solidly on the foundation of God's action and his promise of future action.

*Now to him who is able to do far more abundantly than all that we ask or think, according to the power at work within us, to him be glory in the church and in Christ Jesus throughout all generations, forever and ever. Amen.*
I therefore, *a prisoner for the Lord, urge you to walk in a manner worthy of the calling to which you have been called, with all humility and gentleness, with patience, bearing with one another in love, eager to maintain the unity of the Spirit in the bond of peace.*
*(Ephesians 3:20-4:3, emphasis added)*

The book of Ephesians is six chapters long, and Paul

famously writes it in two halves. Chapters one through three are filled with juicy theological truth about what God has done for us, how he has saved us, and our new identity in Christ. It ends with a great exclamation about God's power at work within us. Then Paul begins chapter four with the words, "I therefore, a prisoner of the Lord ..." Once again he starts a new section utilizing the word therefore. In this case he moves from the theological foundations of God's work and our identity, to the everyday behaviors that we build upon them. The rest of the book, chapters four through six contain these practical instructions

## HOW DOES THIS HELP?

Understanding the presence and function of the word "therefore" helps us build God-confidence in two ways. First, it shows us the flow of thought of the biblical author. It functions as a signpost to help us get at the meaning of the passage. Knowing that Joseph's advice to Pharaoh is solidly built on the interpretation God gave him of Pharaoh's dreams is important. Joseph isn't just being smug or flippant. He believes there is a natural implication to what God has revealed through Pharaoh's dreams. The word "therefore" helps us notice that.

The same is true in the other passages we looked at. The reason the people of Israel could be confident of God's commitment to them, his love and faithfulness, is that God had demonstrated those qualities ever since he chose them to be his people. The reason we can abound in the work of the Lord, being steadfast and immovable, is that God is giving us the victory over death and sin. The three chapters of Ephesians in which Paul gives us practical actions to take rest on the previous three chapters in which God took action to save us and make us new people. Noticing the word "therefore" helps us understand how these things fit together.

Second, it helps us grow in God-confidence by giving us the real, spiritual power to do what Scripture exhorts us to do. So much preaching and teaching today can be summed up in two words: Do better. You need to do this; you gotta do that; you should do the other thing; you oughta do still more stuff. Beating God's sheep in this way is reprehensible. Scripture doesn't give us a long list of to-do's. Scripture gives us deep theological truth to help us build the internal structures of a belief system anchored in who God really is, and who we are in Christ. Even the narrative portions of Scripture are there to illustrate these foundational truths. Only when our hearts are anchored to the foundation of God's character, names, and attributes, and our divine privileges in Christ can we begin to construct the walls, doors, windows, and roof (in other words, the "do better" behaviors).

When all we hear from our pastors and teachers is that we need to do better, we lose confidence. We know we need to do better. I don't know very many believers who aren't frustrated with their ability to act in line with God's Word. But, the power to do better comes from understanding deep within our souls who God is and who he's made us to be in Christ. Without that power, we are doomed to mediocre and hit-and-miss motivation. Recognizing the little word "therefore" helps us understand this.

## AN IMPORTANT NOTE

A number of modern Bible translations have chosen to utilize a theory of translation that can mask the "therefores." In this book I've been quoting from the English Standard Version of the Bible. The ESV translation team tries to stay as close to the original Greek and Hebrew words as is practical. If you look up the same verses in the New International Version or the New Living Translation, you'll see that the word "therefore" isn't always present. That's because these two translations don't focus on the exact words in the original, they focus on the overall meaning. What you end up with is something more like a thought-for-thought translation rather than a word-for-word one.

This doesn't mean you should throw out your NIV or NLT Bibles.[11] Different translations are useful for different things. I own both those translations and often use the NLT in my daily devotional reading. Because it has a different way of thinking about translation, it is often easier to read and the wording can be smoother overall. However, when I'm studying the Bible and want to dig in a bit deeper, I'll use the English Standard Version, New American Standard Bible, or another version that follows a more word-for-word format. By comparing a couple different translations you can get the best of both worlds and come to a deeper understanding of what God wants to say to you.

## CHAPTER 15

# DRILL THE FUNDAMENTALS

The fundamentals of basketball include dribbling, shooting, and passing. Can you bounce the ball without looking at it while running down the court? That's a pretty important skill in basketball. Can you pass it accurately to your teammate? Can you shoot it into the basket consistently, even when the opposing team is guarding you? These are the fundamentals. In order to win, you have to consistently drill the fundamentals. If you've ever been to a professional basketball game, you know that before every game the teams come out and practice the fundamentals. Some of these people are paid millions of dollars per year because their skill level is so high, but just like everyone else, they come out and throw the ball around. They take warm-up shots, and drill the fundamentals.

What are the fundamentals of growing in faith? What skills we need to drill on a regular basis? Here are five fundamentals of God-confidence:

1. The truth about what we fear, and the worst that could happen
2. The truth about ourselves, and who we are in Christ
3. The truth about God, and how he wants to love us
4. The truth about suffering, and the purpose it can serve
5. The truth about the future, and the glory we'll enjoy

## THE TRUTH ABOUT WHAT YOU FEAR

Know the truth about what you fear. Ask yourself this question, "What's the worst that could happen?" Start with the truth about what you're struggling with. Make sure your fear or worry isn't based on false information, made up statistics, or misunderstanding the facts. What is really true in this situation? Then examine what is the worst that could happen. This was hugely helpful to me when I was dealing with fear of flying.

One night I was flying home to Chicago from Orlando at night. It was beautiful outside. I could see for miles as we floated along at 36,000 feet. This was after my Baltimore meltdown (See chapter one). I was just starting to get a handle on my fear of flying, so I'm not totally freaked out, but I'm still kinda scared. I've got the sweaty palms. I'm looking out the window and I think, well, what's the worst that could happen right now?

Interestingly, rather than sending me into a tailspin, asking this question was remarkably freeing. I decided the worst thing that could happen is both engines drop off the plane at the same time and we crash. What would that be like? Well, it would be 10 minutes of terror and then I would see Jesus. If I have to die, that's really not a bad way to go. It's not painful. (The painful thing would be if I crashed and survived, but I wasn't ready to think about that.) But 10 minutes of terror and then I see Jesus? If we all have to go somehow, I'll choose that door, thank you.

That was one of those transformative moments when the pieces start to fit together. I don't want to die necessarily, but thinking about the worst that could happen led me to surrender my life to God in a new way. I said, "Lord, here's my life. If you want me to die in this plane, that's okay, I'll trust you. Oh, and God? Please take care of my wife and daughter." What's the worst that could happen in your situation? As you think about your fear, worry, anxiety, concern, insecurity, or outright panic, what's actually true about it and what's the worst that could happen?

## THE TRUTH ABOUT YOU

What's the truth about you? Who are you, really? What's the truth about who you are in Christ? You are not who the devil says you are when he whispers in your ear. You are not who society says you are. You are not who your spouse says you are, for better or for worse. You are not who your boss says you are. You are not even who you say you are when you tell yourself those horrible things after you do something silly. You are only who Jesus says you are. You are who the Bible says you are. What does it say?

What you believe about yourself is fundamental to

your faith and your ability to grow in God-confidence. It's impossible to be confident if you think you're ugly, stupid, too fat, too skinny, too boring, or too much of a spaz. (It's also impossible to be God confident if you think you're too perfect, but most of us don't really face that problem.) God says you are blessed with every spiritual blessing in the heavenly realms. He says you were chosen by him before he even created the universe. He says you are his adopted child, with all the rights and privileges of an heir, he says you are perfectly accepted in Christ. He says you are righteous and holy, the home of the Holy Spirit, and entrusted with the power that raised Jesus Christ from the dead. And that's all in just one chapter of the Bible (Ephesians 1:1-23). What else does he say about you? You'll have to read about it in his Word.

## THE TRUTH ABOUT GOD

What's the truth about God? Who is he? What is he like? Is he a good God? In what ways is he good? Is he a kindly old grandfather who only wants people to be happy? Is he a great and powerful God? In what ways is he great? Is he loving? Does he personally love you? Is it really true that he wants to use his goodness and greatness on your behalf? If you don't know the truth about God you can't be confident in him. How can you trust someone you don't know anything about? This is why theology is so important. It gives us the foundational truths about God on which we can build the rest of our lives.

There are many great books that can teach you the names of God, Jesus, and the Holy Spirit. I've listed a few in the appendix at the back of this book. Spend some time praying through these names. Get to know God as he really is, not as our fallen world depicts him.

## THE TRUTH ABOUT SUFFERING

What is the truth about suffering? This topic, like many we've addressed, is worthy of several books all on its own, but let's review just one part of it. Why do we suffer?

As we saw earlier in this book, there are four primary causes for suffering. You might suffer as the natural result of your own sin. If you cheat on your tax forms you might go to jail. You might suffer because of someone else's sin. If the IRS agent is trying to boost his audit numbers you may get caught in the crosshairs. If the IRS agent lies, you may have to go to court. You might suffer simply because we live in a broken world. As a believer in Jesus, you might suffer because of your own mistakes. If you screw up your tax forms, you'll have to pay a fine. You didn't sin, nor did anyone else, but none of us are perfect and so suffering ensues. If you live in the Southeast of the United States, you might find yourself in the middle of a hurricane. In this case no one has made any mistakes or sinned, the world we live in is simply broken. Until the new heaven and earth arrive, there will be suffering. Jesus said in this world we will have tribulation (John 16:33). And finally, you might suffer because God is pruning you.

The truth? Suffering exists. At various points in your life you'll experience it, but God has promised that all things will work together for the good of those who love him (Romans 8:28). Your worst suffering is something you will thank God for and rejoice in at some point in the future because he will redeem it and turn it into good. That doesn't mean you have to pretend to be happy, happy, happy all the time. Healthy believers in Christ experience the full range of human emotions, including sadness and anger, but we aren't controlled by them. We must be certain that our suffering is not a surprise to our loving Father, and that our experiences will increase our faith and work for our ultimate good.

## THE TRUTH ABOUT THE FUTURE

What's the truth about the future? The truth is that your destiny is glorious in Christ. One day all things will be summed up in him. Eternity will be an amazingly awesome, wonderful, beautiful, incredible experience forever and ever and ever. Paul says, these little sufferings are like nothing compared to what eternity will be like ( 2 Corinthians 4:17). Take time to meditate on what Scripture says about eternity, about our ultimate home.

## DRILLING OUR FUNDAMENTAL TRUTHS

What's the best way to drill the fundamentals? How do you get the truth about things into your soul? There are two basic steps you can start with. First, begin to intentionally memorize Scripture.

> *Blessed is the man who walks not in the counsel of the wicked, nor stands in the way of sinners, nor sits in the seat of scoffers; but his delight is in the law of the LORD, and on his law he meditates day and night. He is like a tree planted by streams of water that yields its fruit in its*

*season, and its leaf does not wither. In all that he does, he prospers. (Psalm 1:1-3)*

Be the one who meditates on God's Word day and night. Spend more time in the Bible than in front of the television or computer screen. Write down a passage on a 3x5 card and carry it around with you, reading and re-reading it throughout the day. The Navigators organization has a whole system for how to memorize Scripture. Buy it and use it. Hide God's Word in your heart. Allow the Bible to fill your self-talk. Allow Scripture to fill your conversations. Ask questions of others about what they are reading and memorizing. Ask them what they think about the verses you're memorizing. Find a partner and memorize Scripture together.

Second, pray scripture. Fill your conversation with the Lord with his Word. Earlier we saw that we should pray most for what God has promised most. Here's a chance to put that into practice. As you read through the Bible, highlight or make a list of all the promises God gives. Then when it's time to pray, start with those promises. How might your God-confidence improve if you started every morning with a five-minute prayer session focused on God's promises? What would it look like if you also ended your day with another five minutes? Saturate your soul with Scripture and speak it out in prayer.

## CHAPTER 16
# PRACTICE SPECIFIC PLAYS

We understand the game. We've watched game tape, and we've got the fundamentals down. Now we want to focus on some specific plays that we're going to use against our opponent. If we're playing basketball, let's imagine the other team is filled with very tall people and we're very short people. We need to have some specific plays to get around their lanky outstretched arms. Otherwise we're going to get clobbered.

### THOUGHTS ARE THE ENEMY

Here's a specific play for God-confidence: take every thought captive.

> *For the weapons of our warfare are not of the flesh but have divine power to destroy strongholds. We destroy arguments and every lofty opinion raised against the knowledge of God, and take every thought captive to obey Christ, (2 Corinthians 10:4-5)*

Two thousand years after the apostle Paul wrote these words, secular psychologists are starting to see the wisdom in it. They call it "thought replacement." Here's how it works. Get a rubber band and put it on your wrist. Then, every time you have a self-defeating or fearful thought, you snap the rubber band. It's a way of kind of startling yourself into taking notice of what's happening in your mind. SNAP. Oh, wait a second. Airplanes don't just randomly drop out of midair. SNAP. Oh, wait a second. Lightning rarely strikes people, and even when it does, it's rarely fatal. SNAP. Oh, wait a second. This issue is truly out of my control, but I know God is both completely powerful and completely loving and will turn even the most difficult pain into something good. Whenever you're overwhelmed or scared or uncertain, replace the lie with the truth. Take every thought captive, as Paul says, and make it obedient to Christ.

If that's the only thing you did, you'd be amazed how much progress you'd make in three months. Every time you find yourself entertaining thoughts that aren't true, take it prisoner. Replace it with the truth.

What lies might the enemy be trying to make you believe about God, yourself, and your situation? We can anticipate these and respond accordingly. We can plan in advance to have confidence in God. We each have one or more areas of fear that seem to come up again and again for us. We don't have to wait to address it until all of a sudden we're freaking out.

Let's imagine that you're deathly afraid of public speaking. Many people share that fear. They would rather endure an appendectomy without anesthesia than get up in front of a group and give a presentation. "What if I lose my place? What if I forget everything I was going to say? What if I make a mistake? What if my fly is undone? What if everyone laughs at me? What if I trip and fall?" Instead of filling our minds with questions we can't answer or lies we needn't believe, we can create a no-way-I'm-not-going-to-freak-out plan.

Let's start with what we know. We know that no one in human history has ever died from speaking in public. We also know that fear isn't necessarily rational. If we don't monitor our thoughts, it's easy to start getting overwhelmed and freak out about what might happen. What can I plan to do that will keep me focused when my mind tries to hijack my preparation? Maybe I plan to take a short break and pray for a friend or family member. I might make a list of people I know and send a quick email to a different one each time I start to freak out just to let them know how much I care for them. When we're proactively caring for others, it's harder to react with worry.

Another fact we know is that public speaking is an activity many people dread. Part of my plan could be creating or curating resources to encourage others. Leading up to the event, I could post one item each day on Facebook or Instagram to help build the faith of others. I could start a blog with links to other articles and resources people have created that are positive and hopeful.

It seems realistic to think that no matter how emotionally strong I am, the time will come when I'm going to really freak out. Unless I'm totally cut off from my own feelings, at some point I will need to reach out for support. What will I do when that happens? First of all, just recognizing that it will probably happen, that it's natural and okay, is a step in the right direction. We were created to face life in the context of community, especially when we face a crisis, and this situation is no different. Let's make a plan for the time when I can't take it anymore. Who will I turn to? How many people do I know that I can be totally transparent with? Who is in my inner circle that I trust to see me at my absolute worst? How will I connect with them? What will I say? What will I need from them? Do I anticipate that my greatest need will just be a listening ear? Will I want someone to help me fix things? Would a box of chocolates, or a card, or something tangible be appreciated? What if I reached out to a person or two now and talked through how we can be there for each other when we're really falling apart? (Because, let's be honest. We all fall apart sometime, over something.) Do I have the courage to share what I think I'll really need and ask them to help me with it?

## POSITIVE STEPS

Here are some steps we can take to respond to various situations. First, educate yourself. How are airplanes really designed to handle turbulence? How does lightning actually work? Are there really poisonous snakes in Illinois? How many giant anacondas are there in the sewers of my city? What long will I actually have to be speaking in front of people? What steps do other people who have faced my fears taken that have been helpful? The more truth you know about whatever concerns you, the more your thoughts will be based on reality and not your own wild imaginations.

Second, explore what is the worst that could happen. Ask yourself, "What is the absolute worst that could happen?" Then ask, "What am I gonna do about it? Is it in my circle of concern or is it in my circle of influence? If it's in your circle of influence, that's great. You can make a plan for addressing it. But if it's only in your circle of concern, then you focus on prayer and trust that God will do what's right.

Third, use your imagination. Scientists have discovered a weird truth about your brain and emotions. They don't do a good job of distinguishing between imagination and reality. There are several ways we can take advantage of this. Biofeedback is one and mental practice is another. Athletes and musicians engage in mental practice all the time by running scales or plays in their imagination rather than wearing out their bodies on the court or by playing their instrument. A trumpet player may look at her music and think, "What will it feel like to play that note, especially that high E flat that I miss more than I hit? What do I need to do? Okay, I really need to relax into that note. Make sure I've got air pressure, support it from the diaphragm." Then she imagines exactly what it will feel and sound like to give a perfect performance. A basketball player may imagine he's shooting a free throw. How will I set my feet? What will my legs do? What does the perfect release feel like? What will it look like going into the basket and through the net? In this way they can practice or rehearse anywhere they are without moving a muscle.

We can build our confidence in God using the same

techniques. It's called imaginary exposure. The counselor who helped me with my fear of flying taught this to me. I'll share it in the context of flying, but it can be used for pretty much any fear or area of concern.

Start by making a list of everything that's going to happen the day you fly. You get out of bed. You take a shower. You get dressed; you eat; you pack. You put your suitcase into the trunk. You get into the car and drive to the airport. You check in. Then you wait, wait, wait, wait, wait, wait, wait, wait. Write down every single thing that would happen. You get on the plane; there's no overhead bin space left. You're mad. You take your seat; you realize that you're in the wrong seat. Your new seat doesn't recline, and you have to sit next to a two year-old who is already whining. You hear all the clunking that accompanies getting the baggage and food on the plane and the fuel topped off. The flight attendants go through their safety song and dance. (Yes, I know that stuff is important.) You hear the pilot say, "We're currently number nine for take off." Six hours later, you're still on the tarmac. Write everything down that will happens. At the end of step one, I had 11 pages of college ruled notebook paper filled with what would happen before, during, and immediately after the flight.

The second step is to mentally rehearse all the items on the list. Sit in a comfortable chair with the list in your hand. Look at the first couple items. Then close your eyes and go through the motions in your mind of experiencing each one. What will it be like to pack the suitcase? What will I be feeling? How will it feel when I first see the airport from the car window? Imagine the tightening in the pit of your stomach when the first bounce of turbulence hits. My counselor encouraged me to pay special attention to the feelings. Really feel your feelings. Don't try to minimize them. In fact, ramp them up as high as possible. Try to freak yourself out as you practice. At first it would take me an hour or so to do this. I would be exhausted and drenched in sweat by the end. I asked my counselor, "How often do I have to do it?" His answer? Twice a day for at least two weeks before you fly.

You know what I discovered? It helps a lot. In fact, even though I've flown all over the world and no longer consider myself afraid of flying, I still practice imaginary exposure sometimes before I fly. I no longer need an 11 page process, but I spend a few minutes each day for several days before I fly imagining what it will be like to hear weird noises in midair, experience turbulence, and remind myself what I'll do if we suddenly have a drop in cabin pressure.

Two things happen when we practice imaginary exposure. First, we inform our emotions with the truth before we face the scary experience. We drill our minds with what's true beforehand so when we're in the thick of it we can replace the lie of fear with the truth of God's Word. Second, our minds get so used to the experiences involved (each item on the list you made and practiced) and so used to feeling the extreme levels of fear, that it gets used to it. You'll discover as you go through the process that it's a lot harder to ramp up the fear the tenth time you've gone through the exercise than it was the first couple times. By the time you've done it 20 times, it's old hat. Sure, the real life experience will be different, but it won't have the intensity that it did before you started the process.

Educate yourself about what you're worried, fearful, anxious, or insecure about. Ask what is the worst possible outcome. Use your imagination to practice and rehearse what you will do in your most fearful moment. Inform your feelings. Don't allow the lie to hold you ransom to its demands, take every thought captive and make it obedient to the truth in Jesus Christ.

## CHAPTER 17

# MAKE IN-GAME ADJUSTMENTS

In sports, in-game adjustments are the changes to the game plan that are necessary once you begin to see what works and what doesn't. Imagine the opposing team is all tall, and we're all short. We planned some specific plays to shoot from farther away from the basket so the other team can't use their height to block them, but they decide to guard us more closely and actually are blocking the shots. What do we do? How do we adjust in the middle of the game? We might use our greater speed to try to get around the players guarding us and take the ball in for a layup. We might utilize more screens or quick passes to try to get a teammate open for an uncontested opportunity. Whatever we do will have to be different than what we planned, because that's not working.

### TELL IT TO MY HEART

Many believers find they need to make an in-game adjustment related to how they interact with biblical truth.

People often ask me, "How do I move my faith from my head to my heart?" This is an extremely common challenge. We find that we know a lot of facts and stories about God and the Bible, but we struggle to put it into practice because our faith is mostly intellectual. To gain the confidence to trust God with more than our intellectual assent, we need to experience him coming through for us. Many Christians have never been in a position where they need that, or they chalk up God's activity in their lives to coincidence or natural causes. My faith can't grow if every time God works, I believe it's luck or that somehow the universe is smiling on me.

At the same time, it seems that the enemy's plan for believers in what's often called the "first world"[12] is to hold us in a prison of comfort and safety. As long as I can fix my problems with my smarts, my contacts, my money, and my ingenuity, I don't need faith. That's a very middle class problem. In the two-thirds world[13] there's often a small upper class, a large lower class, and hardly any middle class. Spend much time with the majority of people in that environment and you realize they simply don't have the resources to solve the challenges they face.

That doesn't mean there's some extra kind of nobility in being poor, but poverty is a type of stress that can lead to greater faith. We have a lot to learn from our brothers and sisters who are rich in faith due to the poverty they face every day (See James 2:5). As long as I can fix my problems myself, why do I need faith? In order for us to experience God and grow our faith, we need to gently and consistently push ourselves to take God-honoring risks. Without risk there's no need for faith because we're living by sight.

## REAL WORLD EXPERIENCE

I really enjoy Matt Damon in the Jason Bourne movies. In the second movie, The Bourne Supremacy, there's a scene where the old spymaster, Ward Abbot, who helped create Jason Bourne, is being interviewed by the younger upstart, Pamela Landy. She is beginning to unravel the dark secrets behind Abbot's work and questions him about some poor decisions he made. He's getting defensive and very uncomfortable. At one point he looks her in the eye and says, "Pamela, you talk about this stuff like you read it in a book." In other words, you don't have any real-world experience. You're all words and no substance. It's all just an intellectual exercise to you.

Do you know Christians who talk about God like they've only ever read about him in a book? They see Jesus, Napoleon, and Winston Churchill all as historical figures who actually existed. Sure, Jesus is God, but they have no more personal experience of him than they do Napoleon or Winston Churchill. Even more sadly, they don't expect to experience him any more than they expect to experience Napoleon or Winston Churchill. They've never been "in the field" in the middle of the action. They've only ever heard about how God comes through when his people take risks of faith. How many Christians live their lives talking about Jesus—like they've only read about him in a book?

Of course, reading about God in the Bible is essential. We want our souls to be so saturated with Scripture that we can say with the psalmist, "Your Word I have hid in my heart ... (Psalm 119:11). But we forget that the reason God gave us his Word is to connect us to himself.

To return to the basketball metaphor, many of us act like we are the announcers. We study the players and the teams so we can sit on the sidelines and speak intelligently about them to others, but that isn't God's plan. Jesus said that in the same way God sent him into the world, he was now sending us (John 20:21). He doesn't want us on the sidelines talking about the game. He wants us out on the court, winning the game. We do this by taking some risks, and failing, and seeing God come through for us, and picking ourselves up, and trusting God a little more because of his work in our lives, and letting him transform us, and then taking another risk.

## TASTE AND SEE

> *I will bless the LORD at all times; his praise shall continually be in my mouth. My soul makes its boast in the LORD; let the humble hear and be glad. Oh, magnify the LORD with me, and let us exalt his name together! I sought the LORD, and he answered me and delivered me from all my fears. Those who look to him are radiant, and their faces shall never be ashamed. This poor man cried, and the LORD heard him and saved him out of all his troubles. The angel of the LORD encamps around those who fear him, and delivers them. Oh, taste and see that the LORD is good! Blessed is the man who takes refuge in him! (Psalm 34:1-8)*

How do you taste and see that the Lord is good? Let's say you go to a new friend's house for dinner. You don't know this friend very well. Otherwise you would have known to politely decline their invitation for dinner, because you'd have known about their passion for exotic foods. Nevertheless, you find yourself seated at the table and they give you something to eat that you don't recognize. I don't mean you don't recognize the dish, you don't even recognize it as food.

What do you do? Pray you have a big napkin and hope they have a dog? Suddenly feign illness and rush to the nearest Wendy's drive-thru? Or will you taste and see what this mystery food is like? Maybe just take a little bite. This might actually be good, Or it might be the most gross and disgusting thing to ever find its way into your mouth. You decide you're committed to take a little bite and see, just to be polite. Taste and see that the Lord is good. Take a little bite, just a small one. Take a baby step into your fear and see that God, indeed is good. We won't feel like he's faithful until we've experienced that faithfulness firsthand, and that requires taking some risks.

## BABY STEPPING

In my battle against the fear of flying, the very first baby step was using my imagination. I couldn't get on an airplane, yet. I couldn't bring myself to do it. It was too big of a step. But I could sit in my bedroom and imagine what it would be like to fly. For me, that was a risk. Can you pass out because you're so scared? I never did. I got myself really scared though. Start by taking a baby step. What is the first baby step of faith that you can take to head into your fear?

Hall of Fame hockey player Wayne Gretzky said, "You miss every shot you don't take." God started training Israel by showing them his power as evidenced in the plagues he sent on Egypt. Then he brought them through the Red Sea, then provided food and water for them in the wilderness, then they heard his voice and the results of his presence on the mountain. Only after all this did he tell them to enter the Promised Land. He had them take a lot of baby steps first.

> *No man shall be able to stand before you all the days of your life. Just as I was with Moses, so I will be with you. I will not leave you or forsake you. ... Have I not commanded you? Be strong and courageous. Do not be frightened, and do not be dismayed, for the LORD your God is with you wherever you go." (Joshua 1:5, 9)*

This is such a great passage on courage. Moses has died. God appears to Joshua and tells him to get up and lead the people of Israel into the Promised Land. Based on the number of times God repeats himself to Joshua saying, "Be strong and courageous. Don't be afraid," I'm pretty sure Joshua had a little fear about his new assignment. Notice how God encourages him. He doesn't rebuke him. He doesn't mock him for his fear. No, God says he will be with Joshua just like he was with Moses. Through forty plus years in the wilderness, Joshua was Moses' right hand man. He was there when the people ran out of food and God provided. He was there when there was no fresh water and God provided. He was there when the people rebelled and God upheld Moses' leadership. At the time, I'm sure Joshua had no idea he was being groomed to be a great leader of faith, but baby step by baby step that's what God was doing. He was showing him exactly how he would be with him once he was the leader instead of Moses.

I have two suggested baby steps that we can all take regularly. The first baby step is to rejoice and thank. This is from Philippians chapter four. This puts fear in perspective. As we rejoice in God and thank him for all he has done for us, we see our troubles in light of his greatness and goodness.

Then take the second baby step to serve others, to get your mind off yourself. The same counselor who talked to me about imaginary exposure explained to me how serving others can help us build our faith. My family and I were going to be flying to Ireland and then to Bosnia. At the time our daughter, Katelyn, was 11 and we were exploring the possibility of being missionaries in Bosnia. My counselor pointed out that it is a long flight to Ireland. He asked me what my daughter was going to do during the long flight. He suggested that I plan a couple of activities that would be special just for her, but don't tell her. Then, he suggested that when I got really scared, I should pull the special activity out and give it to her, or take that game out and play it with her, or tell her that story. Serving her in some way would help get my mind off of myself. When we serve others, we get our mind off ourselves and take a baby step forward in faith.

Faith was never meant to be alone. It is designed to lead to action. When we take small risks, baby steps, towards

God, and discover that he comes through for us, our faith grows. Put together enough of these baby steps all in a row and suddenly you're walking by courageous faith in Jesus Christ.

## CHAPTER 18

# BUILD ON WHAT WORKS

You did it! You stepped out in faith and saw God come through for you. Feels great doesn't it? It can be exhausting, too. If you're not careful, you'll hide under the bed for two years before you work up the courage to do it again. I know that's what I'm tempted to do.

Don't give in to that temptation. Instead, build on what works. To consolidate your growth in God-confidence you need to take those baby steps again and again. Then you can start facing fear in ever larger ways. Let those baby steps become adult steps. Let those adult steps become giant leaps forward. Let those giant leaps forward become Superman leaping over tall buildings in a single bound.

Any basketball team can have a good game once in a while. The underdog can bring extra focus and energy to the table and beat the number one-ranked team on the right night. However, stringing a season's worth of wins together, requires building on what works. Game tape is watched every week to learn from mistakes. The fundamentals are drilled every day in practice. Specific plays are put together for each unique situation. A successful team builds on what works.

Repetition is required for God-confidence to be sustained. We want to string a season's worth of wins together, one at a time. Musicians warm up with scales and exercises to keep their technique in good form. Basketball players shoot free throws every day. Sales people repeat their pitch again and again. Repetition helps ingrain it, turning it from a one-time fluke into a habit we can count on. So take those risks, those steps of faith again and again and again. You didn't just read about it in a book. It's your real life.

Our emotional memory can be trained just like muscle memory. When you first started brushing your teeth, you had to think carefully about what you were doing to make sure you got every side of every tooth and didn't drool toothpaste down your front. But, now, you barely even think about it. It's automatic. The first time I sat behind the wheel of a car, I had to consciously and intentionally go through the steps of putting on my seatbelt, adjusting the seat and mirrors, and turning the ignition. Now, it's simply a habit.

Just as our brain and muscles can work on their own to perform the patterns necessary to brush out teeth, start the car, type, and a hundred other tasks, our emotions can be trained to be confident in God in a large variety of situations.

> *I will send my terror before you and will throw into confusion all the people against whom you shall come, and I will make all your enemies turn their backs to you.*

*And I will send hornets before you, which shall drive out the Hivites, the Canaanites, and the Hittites from before you. I will not drive them out from before you in one year, lest the land become desolate and the wild beasts multiply against you. Little by little I will drive them out from before you, until you have increased and possess the land. (Exodus 23:27-30)*

When God brought his people into the Promised Land, he did it little-by-little over the course of a generation. He could have simply caused all the people currently living there to pull up stakes and move. He could have just wiped them out so the Israelites only needed to move in and set up shop. But he didn't, for two reasons. First, he didn't want the land to become desolate and wild beasts to multiply. Second, his main priority in this exercise was to build the faith of the people. God is more concerned about your faith than anything else about you. He promised Israel the land, but then said they had to physically go forward and fight for it. Every battle was a new opportunity to trust God for the victory.

God wants our faith and confidence in him to be unshakeable, so he builds it one battle at a time. Anyone afraid to fly can get on an airplane and travel somewhere once. When they arrive at their destination they'll feel like a wet dishrag, and they'll never want to do it again. To be able to get on the plane again and again and again requires us to do something about that fear that works in the long term.

It can feel like the process will never end. You may start, stop, think about giving up, then start again dozens of times.

What's important is that you never stay down. Don't allow the enemy to take you out of the game. Keep at it, bit-by-bit, one baby step at a time.

## MAKING IT PRACTICAL

Here are some practical steps you can take to grow in God-confidence over the long haul.

> *Two are better than one, because they have a good reward for their toil. For if they fall, one will lift up his fellow. But woe to him who is alone when he falls and has not another to lift him up! Again, if two lie together, they keep warm, but how can one keep warm alone? And though a man might prevail against one who is alone, two will withstand him--a threefold cord is not quickly broken. (Ecclesiastes 4:9-12)*

Find a couple of supportive partners to make a team of three. Share with them what you're working on and ask them to pray for you. Make it clear if you want their advice or not. Most people in this situation will give you lots of ideas about what you should do. If you're not looking for that, tell them plainly. Go through the God-confidence Playbook with them so they understand what's at stake. Celebrate every success together with thanksgiving, worship and fun.

The very first time I got on an airplane after that notorious trip to Baltimore was a trip to Sacramento, California. Afterwards my family had a big celebration. They were so proud of me, and that spurred me on to keep going and not give up.

Ensure your progress is measurable by making up tests along the way. My daughter hates hospitals. A combination of fear and bad memories make it difficult for her to visit anyone who is in the hospital. She could monitor her progress by choosing to spend a certain amount of time visiting or volunteering at the hospital. She might set a goal of spending thirty minutes with someone one time a week. Then she could increase that until she really began to feel comfortable. The more you can measure your progress, the more motivated you'll be to stick with it.

Take a final exam. How will you know when you've really licked this thing you're dealing with? Work with your team of three to develop a final exam—a specific, measurable achievement that demonstrates you've grown in God-confidence. Write it down. Plan for it. Pray about it. Accomplish it! Then apply your new God-confidence to another area of concern.

CHAPTER 19

# SHARE YOUR LOVE FOR WINNING

The most inspiring athletes are those who invest in the people around them. They are the ones who make their teammates better, who show up at sports camps to teach kids a love for the game, who spend time helping the less fortunate. You can multiply your hard-won God-confidence by investing in the life of someone else who is struggling with worry, fear, or insecurity. And believe me, at some level, whether we want to admit it or not, we all do.

For some, the thought of mentoring another person is a real stretch. It can be scary just to think about it. But, helping someone walk through the God-confidence process will help solidify your own growing faith, help another find victory over the weight they've been carrying, and deepen your relationship with that person. The joy you'll receive will be well worth the fear you need to walk through to get there. To make it as simple as possible, here are five achievable steps you can take to share your love for winning.

First, identify someone you can help. Start by praying and

asking God to reveal to you someone who, though they may seem like everything is fine on the outside, is struggling with some aspect of fear, worry, or concern. Then begin to observe the people around you through a different set of lenses. Who do you see that backs off from challenges? Who seems confident about most of life, but when a specific topic comes up—kids, school, work, particular activities—they suddenly go quiet? Who has expressed a sense of dissatisfaction with their life or a real desire to grow in their faith? These might be signs that someone is ready to cultivate a more courageous faith in Jesus Christ.

Next, simply broach the subject with the person. You might start by telling a bit of your own story, how you were able to build your faith and beat your fear. Gently ask some questions about their own experience and see if they might be open to considering working together on the process. Inviting them to a God-confidence Seminar or to read this book together could be a great way to test the waters. Of course, there are other resources that you can use as well. Check out the appendix for a list of helpful books and study guides.

Once they have read the book or attended the seminar and have the basic information needed, schedule a recurring time to get together to work through the *God-confidence Game Plan* and pray together. In order to have time between sessions to see real progress, you might suggest meeting every-other-week, or even once a month. Any less than once a month and you'll lose momentum, though, so I wouldn't suggest any less frequent than that.

Once you start meeting, the game plan can guide

you through the specifics of what to talk about. Share examples of what you did, what steps you took, where you struggled. You don't need to tell the person what to do. Ultimately they are responsible for creating their own plan and implementing it, but sharing your own victories and challenges can help them picture what is possible. At some point you might suggest the person talk with someone else who has completed the process to gain additional insights into how God has worked to build faith in his people.

Finally, make sure you celebrate each small victory. Even if every step forward is followed by a half step backward, acknowledging and celebrating progress will help to confirm new habits and ways of thinking. Before you know it, your friend will see how far they've come and be eager to continue on. Soon they'll be sharing their own love for winning!

## STEPS TO SHARING YOUR LOVE FOR WINNING:

1. Identify a friend you can help.
2. Invite them to join you on the journey.
3. Attend a God-confidence Seminar or read this book together.
4. Meet regularly to work step-by-step through the *God-confidence Game Plan*.
5. Celebrate each victory, especially when they are ready to help someone new start the process in their own lives.

## CHAPTER 20
# THE 10-STEP GAME PLAN TO GOD-CONFIDENCE

Here's what the entire God-confidence process looks like.

1. *You face something scary.*

   It may be a fear of flying or the anxiety associated with shipping your firstborn off to college, or the possibility of bad news from the doctor. We each have our own unique concerns. Whatever it is, it throws us off our game. It distracts us from the life of joy and peace God wants for us.

2. *You feel the fear.*

   It's possible that the fear is overwhelming and tangible. Your palms sweat; your heart starts trying to beat on the outside of your body; your breathing comes in short gasps of desperation. Or, it may feel more subtle. You may not realize for days that you've been distracted and worried about an issue. Then one night as you lie in bed you realize that your neck and shoulders are as hard as granite and all you can think about is whether or not your mom will be okay in the new nursing home. Recognizing the fear is an essential step.

3. *Inventory your feelings.*

   Where did these feelings come from? What beliefs are they based on? Are those beliefs true? Are they reasonable?

   My dad lives in Arizona, a three-hour flight and two-hour car ride away from me. At 82 he's in very good health, but he still lives alone in his house and drives his car by himself. Sometimes I get concerned that something will happen to him and no one will discover it for days. Then I remember that he has a good friend in town who he talks or texts with several times a day. My fear isn't based in reality. In step three we diagnose what's going on with our feelings so we can take the best action.

4. *Educate your feelings with the truth about what you fear.*

   The truth is that flying is by far the safest way to travel. The truth is that no one has ever died from public speaking. The truth is those people you think are laughing about you across the room probably haven't even noticed you. Our feelings aren't bad, but they often aren't very smart. They need to be educated.

5. *Inform your feelings of God's goodness and greatness.*

   Rehearse the truth about who God is and what he's already done for you. Memorize his attributes, names, and aspects of his character. Read passages from Scripture that point out these truths. Ephesians chapters one through three, Colossians chapters one and two, and pretty much any of the psalms are good places to spend some time.

6. *Regardless of how you feel, act based on faith, not feelings.*

    It may take all your strength to do so. You may need to call your team of three and have them pray you through it over the phone as you do it. Don't allow the fear to control your actions. Remember what we most revere is what we give power to in our lives. Commit yourself now to only revering God and only allowing him to control your life.

7. *God carries you through.*

    Seven is the perfect number. The seventh action is not something you do, but something God does. He carries you through. It wasn't luck, circumstance, or coincidence. It was God. The creator and sustainer of the universe looked at little 'ole you, loved you, and decided to use his incredible power on your behalf. In retrospect it's easy to explain these moments away. Don't give in to that temptation. Find a way to remember it.

    Earlier I related the story of when a home health nurse came to visit us. She encouraged us greatly during a very dark time. It would have been easy to write off as coincidence, but instead, we got a glass jar, filled it with twelve small rocks[14] and kept it on the shelf in our living room. It was a way for us to ensure that we would remember how God had been faithful to us and to gain courage and God-confidence when we faced the next difficulty in our lives. We still have that jar full of rocks, and it still sits in a prominent place in our home.

8. *Our confidence in God's greatness and goodness grows.*

    Even if just a little bit, our confidence will grow because of the experience. Remember in chapter four we discovered that confidence requires stress. This is the point at which that stress pays off. When you've done the necessary work of taking risks, informing your emotions, acting in faith, and seeing God move, it takes your confidence to the next level.

9. *Transfer this new confidence to other areas of life.*

    While there are many types of concern, fear, anxiety, and insecurity, they can all be bested in the same way. Take another step of faith. Do it again. Take a little bit bigger risk. We need to continue to grow in God-confidence and faith every day of our lives. We can stop when we reach heaven because at that point we won't need faith. We'll be forever in Jesus' physical presence and will be living by sight.

10. *Share your experience of God-confidence with others.*

    When you help others experience the same victory you have, you multiply the impact of your experiences and effort. Don't allow all your hard work to be only for yourself. Leverage it for the benefit of others. This is part of what Jesus' meant when he said that the good soil bears fruit and yields thirty, sixty, or one-hundredfold (Matthew 13:23). We can multiply the effectiveness of our efforts by sharing with others.

Most of us will not get a free, miraculous ticket out of fear, worry, and insecurity, and into God-confidence. That's because the most important thing that God cares about in your life is your faith, and faith is built over time. That's one of the main reasons why he allows hardship into our lives (1 Peter 1:3-7). Remember that God didn't drive the enemies of Israel out all in one year. God promised them the land, and then they had to fight for it. In the same way, God promises us joy and freedom from anxiety, but we experience it as we fight for it.

I pray that you will not grow weary in the battle, that you will surround yourself with a few people you can trust who will uphold you with God's truth, that you will take the baby steps of faith and experience God's wonderful power and love again and again. To him be all the glory. Amen.

## APPENDIX
# ADDITIONAL RESOURCES

### ON OUR IDENTITY IN CHRIST

Cloud, Henry., Townsend, John. *How People Grow: What the Bible Reveals about Personal Growth.* United States: Zondervan, 2004.

Giovannetti, Bill. *Grace Rehab: The Power of Labeling Yourself the Way God Labels You.* United States: Endurant Press, 2015.

Coleman, Adaline., Giovannetti, Bill. *Grace Rehab Study Guide: The Power of Labeling Yourself the Way God Labels You.* United States: Endurant Press, 2015.

Cloud, Henry., Townsend, John. *How People Grow: What the Bible Reveals about Personal Growth.* United States: Zondervan, 2004.

Kraeuter, Tom. *Your Identity Has Been Stolen: Discovering Who You Really Are in Christ.* Hillsboro: Training Resources, Inc. , 2019.

## ON FREEDOM FROM FEAR

Arthur,Kay.*Breaking Free from Fear: A 6-Week, No-Homework Bible Study.* United States: Crown Publishing Group, 2012.

Giovannetti,Bill. *Grace Breakthrough: Exploding the Lies that Wound Your Confidence and Joy.* N.p.: Endurant Press, 2016.

Barcanic, John. *The Road to Freedom: A 12-Week Study.* N.p., 2019

## ON KNOWING GOD

Packer,J. I..*Concise Theology: A Guide to Historic Christian Beliefs.* United States: Tyndale House Publishers, Incorporated,2011.

Packer, J. I.. *Knowing God.* United States: InterVarsity Press, 2011.

Tozer, A. W.. *The Knowledge of the Holy: The Attributes of God.* India: General Press, 2019.

Evans,Tony. *The Power of God's Names.* United States :Harvest House Publishers, 2014.

Evans, Tony. *Praying Through the Names of God.* United States: Harvest House Publishers, 2019.

Keller, Timothy. *The prodigal God.* United States: Dutton, 2008.

Spurgeon, Charles H.. *The Promises of God: A New Edition of the Classic Devotional Based on the English Standard Version.* United States: Crossway, 2019.

# ACKNOWLEGMENTS

To Jennifer Brody, who patiently edited the first draft of this book and didn't laugh at all my errors.

To Lyn Barcanic for her inspiration and motivation to keep going when it got difficult.

To my friends at South Park Church who allowed me to experiment on them in the God Confidence Seminar, which eventually became the foundational material for this book.

To Kathy Barcanic who has never laughed at my dreams and aspirations and, though she may not always understand them, consistently supports and encourages me.

# ABOUT
# JOHN BARCANIC

John Barcanic helps change-makers turn vision into action, and action into transformation. As the Founding Director of Intersekt, John knows that both personal and community transformation occur best in the context of healthy, authentic relationships.

A sought after speaker, coach, and consultant, his skills have delivered results for a broad array of organizations in more than 10 countries on four continents He is recognized for his ability to make deep theological truth readily understandable and immediately applicable.

John is an ordained pastor, certified leadership coach, and jazz pianist. When he's not speaking, coaching, or consulting, you can find John at a café in his hometown of Chicago playing piano with his jazz trio, reading a gripping novel, or debating whether or not people can fly in heaven.

# ABOUT INTERSEKT

Are you one of those people who sometimes feels like you're on the outside looking in? You see things differently than others.

Change seems to follow you around like an adoring kid brother, whether you want it to or not. You can't help but see how things could be different, better. You know change is difficult, but you seem to be willing to pay the price for a better future when others only want to hold on to the status quo.

You're curious, and you often start sentences with the words, "What if ..." What if Christians took Jesus at his word? What if we were willing to sell all we have and give the money to the poor? What if we loved our neighbors, and our enemies, with Christ's sacrificial love? What if we had the boldness and the meekness to share the gospel like the apostles did? What if we could change? That's what you are: a change-maker.

Intersekt was formed to help change-makers join

God's mission in the world. It's hard to be the voice of dissatisfaction, the one constantly calling for revolution. (At least it feels like revolution to those around you.) We want to see your ideas realized. The world needs you, your vision, and your energy. We can help you turn vision into action and action into transformation.

It starts by living at the intersection of God's Word and our world. It continues by taking steps of faith every day. It doesn't end until our communities are transformed by God's grace.

Intersekt is a division of *Innovative Ministries International*.

Discover more at www.intersekt.org.

## ENDNOTES

1. No one can read your mind. It's a common misconception that "If you really loved me you'd understand me." Love and relationships are hard work. We need to be willing to speak up and ask for what we need.

2. Someone asked, "What if I don't feel anything?" You may struggle to feel glad, sad, mad, or scared. You may instead feel numb, which is actually the absence of emotion. There are many reasons this might happen. You may simply be very tired. Or you may be struggling with depression—sadness over a long period of time. Everyone experiences numbness once in a while. But, if this struggle continues for very long, please see a doctor. It may be a sign that something more serious is happening.

3. A.W. Tozer, *The Knowledge of the Holy* (New York: HarperCollins, 1978), 1.

4. For those who aren't aware, Michael Jordan played for the Chicago Bulls from 1984-1993 and from 1995-2001. During that time he led the team to six NBA championships. He was a pretty good player.

5. Ben Bernanke, former head of the Federal Reserve, quoted in *CNNBusiness*. https://money.cnn.com/2014/08/27/news/economy/ben-bernanke-great-depression/index.html

6. It's important to note that the spiritual realm we interact with while alive is different from the place where departed souls go when they die. Your Aunt Mabel isn't floating around in the ether trying to send you messages via some spirit medium.

7. The concept of a circle of concern and circle of influence

was originated by Stephen Covey in his excellent book *The 7 Habit of Highly Effective People*.

8. I realize that through prayer God may work in situations beyond our circle of influence. However, that actually proves the point that I am not able to directly influence those matters. Please don't misunderstand me. I am all in favor of prayer.

9. Though I'm aware of the various theories of time, let's keep our discussion to how the typical human experiences it for the sake of this discussion.

10. Abraham's son Isaac, grandson Jacob, and great-grandson Joseph (three generations) all lived in the land promised to Abraham. Jacob's family all moved to Egypt to avoid a famine and remained there, growing and multiplying, for 400 years.

11. The very popular Message Bible is not a translation, but rather a paraphrase. It can be helpful for getting a more modern flavor for how the author may have sounded had he spoken today. However, I wouldn't recommend it as your go-to Bible in most situations.

12. Countries referred to as "first world" are generally those countries that are highly developed, industrialized, and westernized. Some prefer the term "global north" as many of these countries are in the northern hemisphere.

13. The two-thirds world is a term referring to South America, Asia, Africa, and Oceana. Roughly two-thirds of the world's population live in these regions.

14. Piling up rocks as a way of remembering God's faithfulness is a regular thing in the Old Testament. See, for instance, Joshua 4:1-11.

www.ingramcontent.com/pod-product-compliance
Lightning Source LLC
Chambersburg PA
CBHW021945290426

**44108CB00012B/969**